SKI JUMPING
—— IN THE ——
NORTHEAST

SKI JUMPING
IN THE
NORTHEAST

Small Towns and Big Dreams

ARIEL PICTON KOBAYASHI

FOREWORD BY FORMER U.S. SKI JUMPING HEAD COACH LARRY STONE

THE
History
PRESS

Published by The History Press
Charleston, SC
www.historypress.com

Front cover, top: Photograph by Savage Frieze taken in Salisbury,
Connecticut, 2021. Jumper: Cameron Forbush; *bottom*: Warren Chivers
Archive. Jumper: Birger Ruud, competing in the 1932 Lake Place
Olympics (photographer unidentified).
Back cover, bottom: Photograph by Cooper Dodds, taken of the 120-meter ski
jump in Lake Placid, 2015; *inset*: Warren Chivers Archive.

First published 2021

Manufactured in the United States

ISBN 9781467148160

Library of Congress Control Number: 2021945854

Notice: The information in this book is true and complete to the best of our
knowledge. It is offered without guarantee on the part of the author or The
History Press. The author and The History Press disclaim all liability in
connection with the use of this book.

CONTENTS

Contents

CONTENTS

FOREWORD

Having grown up in the little Northwest Connecticut town of Salisbury where I learned to ski through the woods and jump on the ski jumps that sprouted up in so many backyards and hills in town, I am delighted to write the foreword to a new book written by a fellow Salisbury Winter Sports Association coach who became as enamored with the sport as I have been.

We all dreamed of becoming like our heroes: the Satres, Sherwoods and the Tokles, but I never dreamed that in following their exploits I would eventually get to ski and coach on those legendary ski jumps so far away from the Salisbury hills: from the U.S. hills mentioned in this book to the Black Forest, Austria, Slovenia, Norway, Sweden, Finland, Russia and even Japan.

It all happened because of the good fortune that several Norwegian immigrants to the New World settled in the Salisbury area and many other areas that reminded them of the Norwegian countryside. They brought with them a whole culture of Nordic skiing, which flourished in the small towns of the northern United States. In this well-written and thoughtful book, Ariel Kobayashi takes us on a journey through the origins of this esoteric, romantic sport to the huge spectacles of giant ski flying hills where current elite ski jumping athletes literally fly distances over eight hundred feet down the side of a mountain.

What I appreciate in this book is that Ariel has attempted and succeeded in doing more than just following the progress of the sport and its ups and downs, technically and culturally. She has explained (using her words) "the spirit of ski jumping at a more personal and local level." What is it about this sport that has captivated so many of us and driven us to incorporate it into lifelong involvement? Ariel has felt and understands it as well as anyone, and I am happy that she has captured the "Spirit of Ski Jumping" in her new book.

Larry Stone
Former U.S. Head Coach for the Men's and Women's Ski Jumping Teams
Lake Placid Head Ski Jumping Coach 1988–2008
Former Jumper and 1982–1988 Coach
for Salisbury Winter Sports Association

ACKNOWLEDGEMENTS

This book began in 2019 as a yearlong senior project while finishing my history degree at SUNY Purchase, and I want to thank my advisor, Dr. Lisa Keller, for her expert guidance and support through that process. I also want to thank my interviewees: Mat Kiefer, Larry Stone, Mark Levasseur, Walter Malmquist, Mark Picton, Art Tokle, Chris Jones, Erling Heistad and Carey Fiertz.

I want to thank Cameron Forbush for his beautiful jump in Salisbury during Jumpfest 2021, which made the cover of this book, and many thanks to the talented photographer Savage Frieze, who captured Cameron's jump so beautifully and generously allowed me to use his photograph on the cover. I am incredibly grateful to Larry Stone for writing the foreword to this book, as well as all those who helped me with information and photographs, including Barry Webber with the Norfolk Historical Society, Gerry Kassel with the Colebrook Historical Society, the Williams College Special Collections, Sarah Currie with the Williamstown Historical Museum, the Bethel Historical Society, the Conway Historical Society, Walter Nadeau with the Moffett House Museum, the Salisbury Association and Sarah Morrison, Barbara Chalmers with the Sunapee Historical Society, the New England Ski Museum, Louise McCormack with the Plymouth Historical Society, Danielle Rougeau with the Middlebury College Special Collections and Archives, Paul Haggett with the St. Lawrence University Archives, the Newport Historical Society, Dennis Breton of the Chisholm Ski Club and Rumford Historical Society, Joanne Olson with the Sandisfield Historical

Society, Jeremy Davis with the New England Lost Ski Areas Project, Matthew Thorenz with the Moffat Library of Washingtonville, Gail Wiese with the Norwich University Archives and Special Collections, Nancy Woolley with the Rochester Historical Society, the Rosendale Library, Saralyn Smith with the Kennett Alumni and Oliver Weeger with skisprungschanzen.com, as well as Kenny Barker, Dan Warner, Matt Bannerman, Jay Rand, Lisa Kling, Scott Halvorson, Tom Dodds, Kathleen Doyle, Betty Ann Heistad, Bob Schmid, Sean Hurley, Cheryl Summerton, Jon Paul Nelson, Becky Pingree, Neal Estano, Jim Cormier, Mike Stowell, Tom and Robert Remington, Gil Villahermosa and Tara Geraghty-Moats.

I leaned heavily on the Historical Newspaper Database at SUNY Purchase to find articles, many of which were from the *New York Times*. Books that were very helpful include Tim Ashburner's *The History of Ski Jumping*, Harold "Cork" Anson's *Jumping Through Time: A History of Ski Jumping in the United States and Southwest Canada*, Marit Stub Nybelius and Annette R. Hofmann's *License to Jump! A Story of Women's Ski Jumping*, Tom and Robert Remington's *We Jumped*, Roland Huntford's *Two Planks and a Passion: The Dramatic History of Skiing*, Ted Bays's *Nine Thousand Years of Skis: Norwegian Wood to French Plastic*, John Fry's *The Story of Modern Skiing* and E. John B. Allen's *From Skisport to Skiing: One Hundred Years of an American Sport*.

A huge thanks goes to Cooper Dodds for making available the Warren Chivers photograph archive to me, which Cooper had previously digitized. I am also grateful to him for allowing me to use many of his own photographs for this book. Likewise, I am extremely thankful to Ted Chivers for letting me use so many photos from the Warren Chivers Archive and to Walter Malmquist for compiling a list of as many of the northeastern jumps, active and dormant, as he could find. His list helped me organize Part II of this book. Thanks also to Mike Kinsella and the talented staff of The History Press.

Lastly, I especially want to thank my mom, Alison Gilchrist, for her expert help editing this book; my dad, Mark Picton, for igniting my love for skiing years ago and for helping me brainstorm; and my brother, Cameron. To my husband, Adam, thank you for your constant support and belief in me, and to Wes, who is the brightest light in my life and allowed me to work on this book while he napped on my chest.

PART I

1

INTRODUCTION

The patch of ice at the top of the twenty-meter ski jump seemed to angle off into the dark, steep woods that pitched down toward the frozen swamp below. My icy nine-year-old fingers fumbled with stiff bindings that wouldn't give, and my heavy, old wooden jumping skis kept skittering away before I could fasten the bindings. Finally ready, I spread both arms wide to brace myself on the two knotty posts at the top of the jump and beheld the steep, icy inrun. Heart clenched, I willed myself to inch forward. Then I heard the familiar, comforting voice of my coach calling up to me, "Ready, Ariel?" I was ready.

If you drive down Main Street of Salisbury, Connecticut, you might miss the sign by the library that says "Salisbury Ski Jump" with an arrow pointing down a small road. You might drive all the way through town and on toward Great Barrington and the Berkshires and never even realize that just outside of Salisbury's small town center is a towering ski jump and with it an almost one-hundred-year tradition that is an essential part of the town's history and spirit. The same phenomenon is possible in Brattleboro, Vermont, where a giant jump rises from a big field outside of town, and in Hanover, New Hampshire, there is a well-hidden cluster of jumps that you will never "just stumble upon"—you really have to know where to go to find them, and even then, you might not find them. The truth is, ski jumping is an obscure sport in this country. There are just a few hundred ski jumpers in the United States and only eleven active jumping programs in the Northeast. But that hasn't always been the case.

At one point, there were well over one hundred jumping sites in the Northeast, many of which had multiple hills.[1] The number is likely much higher than that, too, because jumping was so popular that small backyard ski jumps were ubiquitous in many towns in the Northeast during much of the twentieth century. While writing this book, I often heard people mention ski jumps that I had never heard of: behind the town garage, or next to the elementary school, or behind their friends' houses. Today, all but a few of those jumps are gone—they've been taken back by nature or bulldozed and replaced with condominiums or shopping centers. However, for a sport that has struggled in the United States for several decades, there is a strong and intangible draw to ski jumping that has the ability to gather communities together to keep the sport going. With this book I hope to paint a picture of the cultural, social and organizational history and identity of ski jumping, the obstacles the sport has faced and why it prevails in America.

WHAT IS SKI JUMPING?

Ski jumping is a sport in which you ski down a steep, snow-covered ramp called an inrun in a low "inrun position" and push off the ground at the takeoff, which is sloped slightly downward. You then fly through the air in an aerodynamic position—leaning forward over the skis, which are positioned in a "V" underneath you so as to create the surface area that will catch the most air. As you glide through the air and clear the knoll, which is the flat or gently sloping area just below the takeoff before the hill plunges steeply downward, you remain relatively close to the ground, following the shape of the hill you will eventually land on. The slope is called the landing hill. Then, the slope flattens out, and the progression from steep to flat is called the transition. The flat area that you eventually come to a stop in is the outrun.[2] The inrun of the jump can be built into a tower or trestle, sometimes towering over the rest of the landscape. Other times, the entire ski jump is built into a hillside. The profile of the landing hill matches the trajectory of a perfect ski jumping flight.

WHY DO PEOPLE SKI JUMP?

Some point to the thrill and excitement of jumping; some explain that it's just simply fun. I think it's the particular feeling a jumper gets in the air—it's

Kai McKinnon on Salisbury's sixty-five-meter hill, 2021. *By Cooper Dodds.*

as close as you can get to flying. "It's thrilling and daring," added my father, Mark Picton, "and when you watch it, it's beautiful. The idea of leaving the earth and soaring through the air is in almost everyone's dreams. It's in the subconscious, and here's a place in the real world where you can try that out; it's designed for that…but I think it's as much about the feeling of doing it as it is about belonging to a group of people who do it."[3]

Former jumper Walter Malmquist described the feeling:

> *Time dilates because your heart rate slows down.…When you explode off the takeoff into your flying position and you rotate over the knoll, the world has slowed down and you can see more things than you could see if you were standing still. At sixty miles per hour, the world expands.…In that moment, you're seeing things much more closely. Everything is magnified; time stands still until you put your front foot forward with a perfect landing, and then you put two hands up as you go through the transition, and the crowd erupts. That's what ski jumping can present.[4]*

Tara Geraghty-Moats on Lake Placid's ninety-meter hill during the summer of 2017. *By Ariel Kobayashi.*

I began ski jumping in 1999 at age nine with the Salisbury Winter Sports Association (SWSA) in Salisbury, Connecticut. I jumped until I was fifteen and took part in two Junior Olympic competitions in 2004 and 2005 in Steamboat Springs, Colorado, and Anchorage, Alaska (more recently known as the Junior Nationals and Junior Championships). With the increasingly limited options for training in Connecticut at the time, due to a lack of snow and no coach, I found it hard to excel at the sport and quit in 2005. At that point, I was the only remaining jumper at my club.

In 2015, I came back to watch the ski jumping event in Salisbury and decided to try jumping again. Living in Vermont at the time, I began jumping and helping out with snowmaking and hill prep at the Lebanon Outing Club in Lebanon, New Hampshire. That winter I also worked with SWSA to help prepare for the Junior Nationals, to be held on the seventy-meter jump there. During that week, Kenny Barker, SWSA's president, asked me to be the next SWSA ski jumping coach. I gladly accepted, coaching young ski jumpers on the twenty- and thirty-meter hills for the next four years. Being a coach reacquainted me with the ski jumping community and later inspired me to dig into the history of ski jumping with this project.

ABOUT *SKI JUMPING IN THE NORTHEAST*

The book is made up of two sections: Part I is a history of ski jumping, which began in Norway, and traces the sport's development in the United States and the northeastern states in particular. Part II is composed of brief histories of each active jump in the Northeast as well as many of the larger (over fifty meter) jumps that no longer exist. The hills I chose to write about represent only a fraction of the multitude of hills that once existed; this is not meant to be a complete inventory of jumps in the Northeast, nor is it an exhaustive history of ski jumping. Instead, I chose to capture the spirit of ski jumping at a more local, personal level.

HOW SKI JUMPS ARE MEASURED AND SCORED

Ski jumps are measured in meters, not feet, and the size of a ski jump corresponds to the measurement from the takeoff to the farthest distance a jumper can safely jump before the hill flattens out. The size of a ski jump is either referred to by its "K Point" or "Hill Size." The K Point of a hill is the farthest distance a jumper can land before the hill begins to flatten out; at this point, the hill is still at its steepest. The Hill Size is a measurement farther down the hill and is calculated based on certain hill data. The Hill Size is the farthest point on the hill that a jumper can still safely and reasonably land. The jumping community now officially uses the Hill Size (HS) measurement to refer to the size of a hill, such as an HS70.[5] The same jump can also be referred to as a K65, where K refers to the K Point. In this work, I often refer to a jump by its K Point or, in the case of a K65, simply call it a sixty-five-meter jump, because many of the jumps I mention are still commonly referred to following that system.

A ski jumper is scored on their style as well as on their distance. Style points are based on three components of a ski jumper's execution of the jump: the flight, landing and outrun. A jumper's flight should be controlled, balanced and use the air pressure effectively to create the maximum flight potential, using the "combination of body and ski to build an entire flying system."[6] Their landing should be in the Telemark style, landing with one foot in front of the other, and should be steady, controlled and without squatting or touching the ground with the hands or back. The jumper should ski into the outrun demonstrating full control.[7]

2

A NORWEGIAN SPORT TAKES FLIGHT

For thousands of years, skiing was a means of transportation in snow-covered regions of northern Europe, Siberia and Russia. Skis enabled travel over otherwise impassable terrain, making communication and trade possible in inhospitable environments. Roland Huntford, a scholar of polar history and exploration, refers to skis as "one of the few Stone Age implements handed down to us in their original form.…The origins of skiing are bound up with the emergence of modern man."[8] In Finland, 3,500-year-old wooden skis have been discovered in peat bogs. Petroglyphs from 5000 BC illustrate the use of skis, and medieval texts identify groups of nomads on skis called Skridfinns, who traversed the icy north from the sixth to the sixteenth centuries.[9] A skiing god and goddess, Ullr and Skadi, have presided in Norse folklore for centuries.[10] In the eighteenth and nineteenth centuries, the Norwegian military used skis to transport troops in the winter, and soldiers kept boredom at bay by sliding down hills on their skis.[11]

Ancient skis have been found in Europe and Asia, but not in America. Huntford explains that when European colonists arrived in America, "the snowshoe was part of Indian tribal culture,"[12] but skis were not: the "deep, loose [snow] variety of the North American forests and the Great Plains needed the snowshoe. The more compact form that mantled steppe and tundra favoured the ski.…The ski belonged to the Old World alone. It existed where the winters were long and stable, with consistent snow."[13]

Ski jumping's birth and the emergence of skiing as a modern sport coincided with the mid-nineteenth-century's Industrial Revolution and a shifting attitude toward nature. In America as well as Europe, as the land exploded with the noise and grit of expanding cities, many people who once worked from their own homes, farms and shops moved to jobs in dark, filthy factories, utterly detached from the outdoors. Over time, those who could afford to do so began to rediscover the value of being out of doors and to seek out untouched, wild landscapes for recreation or more contemplative experiences.

In the United States, a new importance was placed on conserving natural spaces and promoting the public use of land. Social reformers of the mid-1900s encouraged the designation of urban parks, which were seen to have restorative and salubrious effects on the inhabitants of crowded urban places. Central Park in New York City, designed in 1857 by Frederick Law Olmsted and Calvert Vaux, was the first among many such places to provide an escape from city life.[14] Congress designated the first National Park of Yellowstone in 1872[15] in an attempt to preserve some of the unique natural spaces of the country. In the decades that followed, early environmentalist John Muir pushed for the designation of national parks in the West, and Woodrow Wilson established the National Park Service in 1916.[16] Moreover, organizations devoted to public wellness were established during this period, with a focus on recreation and physical activity.[17] A renewed focus on natural spaces prompted excitement about their use in outdoor pursuits like skiing and ski jumping.

In the late nineteenth century, outdoor-focused clubs and organizations began to appear. In the Northeast, an outdoor social scene emerged; hiking and camping became popular, and colleges formed ski clubs and built wilderness cabins in the mountains and lakes regions of New England and the Adirondacks.[18] The Appalachian Mountain Club, established in 1876, was devoted to preserving wilderness and facilitating its public use by cutting hiking trails and setting up camps and cabins.[19] That organization became an early supporter of winter recreation and skiing in the early 1900s.[20] This shift to outdoor pursuits in America was embedded in a cultural attitude that was, by the turn of the twentieth century, ready to welcome the new sport of ski jumping. Long before becoming an American sport, however, ski jumping belonged to the Norwegians.

By the end of the nineteenth century, skiing had become an important part of Norwegian life. Ski jumping began as just one component of a Norwegian overland ski tour or commute: skiing was the means for travel from one place to another in the winter, and without dedicated trails between farms and towns, ski jumping transpired as an efficient way of clearing obstacles on the way down a hill.[21]

Sondre Nordheim, circa 1880. *Wikimedia Commons.*

In the 1860s, a simple innovation in ski bindings revolutionized skiing and made ski jumping viable as a sport. Until the 1860s, skis were strapped to the feet by a simple toe strap, but when Sondre Nordheim, born in 1825 in Morgedal, a small town in the Telemark region of Norway, invented the heel strap, effectively fastening a skier's boot down to the ski, the sport of skiing was forever changed. The heel strap gave skiers control of their skis, allowing them to turn and stop with ease and retain control while airborne.[22] Nordheim demonstrated the use of his new technology, astounding a crowd by skiing beautifully through the air and landing victoriously at the first official ski jumping competitions in Telemark and Christiania, Norway, in 1866 and 1868.[23]

Nordheim came from a small village in rural Norway, yet he became a national icon, Huntford argues—something Norway could be proud of: "Like most Telemark skiers, Nordheim was poor and belonged to the land. He scratched a living as a country carpenter making spare parts for the handlooms that were still a staple of almost every farm.…Insignificant in a crowd, on a pair of skis he came into his own."[24] While he eventually moved to the United States with his family, Nordheim would be remembered in Norway as the "King of Skiing."[25]

Over the next decade, ski jumping progressed into a competitive sport. More jumps were built in Telemark, Christiania, Holmenkollen and other small communities in Norway, and with new jumps came the formation of ski clubs and manufacturers across the country.[26] By the mid-nineteenth century, the Norwegian phrase *Ski-Idraet* had come to embody an important but difficult-to-define idea. Central to the Norwegian tradition of ski jumping, ski historian E. John B. Allen describes Idraet as "the idea of striving [through skiing] to perfect the individual soul as well as the body, and ideally would develop 'the physical and moral strength of nations.'"[27]

In the late 1800s, skiing's popularity took off. In 1888, Fridtjof Nansen, a Norwegian explorer, scientist and diplomat, won fame that popularized skiing worldwide when he became the first to ski across Greenland, as well as making an ambitious attempt on skis to reach the North Pole a few years later:[28]

*He set off for Greenland with specially designed skis and sleeping bags....
The proposed four month trip became a grueling year-long ordeal, as the
men hauled sledges in temperatures that froze their noses, larynxes and even
their urine....The party crossed Greenland for the first time, without loss
of human life, and was rewarded with some 50,000 people turning out on
the Oslo quayside to greet the men.*[29]

Nansen's Greenland expedition on skis sparked international excitement
for the sport.[30] Soon, the skiing craze spread across Europe and crossed the
ocean to America.

In North America as early as the eighteenth century, Siberian fur traders
used skis to cross snow-covered Alaskan terrain to maintain their traps.[31]
In the 1850s during the California Gold Rush, miners held ski races down
mountain chutes outside of mining towns in the West,[32] and postal workers
delivered mail on skis through mountain passes to snowbound towns. During
the 1850s, "Snowshoe" Thompson delivered mail on skis over a ninety-mile
stretch through mountain passes from Carson Valley, Nevada, to Placerville,
California.[33] Thompson, whose name was Jon Torsteinsson Rue, was also
from Telemark, Norway, and he is often credited with bringing skiing to
the American West.[34] Though "alpine" skiing, the freeform method of
skiing down hills while making turns, gained popularity, ski writer John Fry
argues that "Norwegians, in particular, clung to the belief that the Nordic
competitions of cross-country and jumping were the only true tests of skiing.
The new alpine races were seen as possibly impure."[35]

From the 1860s to the 1920s, Norwegians immigrated to America in
large numbers. Ski jumping, a cultural marker, came with them.[36] Economic
hardship and religious circumstances contributed to the surge in Norwegian
immigration to the United States: in particular, an 1860s famine, a failure
in herring fisheries in the 1880s and, in the 1890s, a shipping depression.[37]
In America, Norwegians sought work as sailors and farmers and scrambled
for land with the Homestead Act in 1862, which offered 160 acres of land
to settlers in the West. Attracted to areas of America that most resembled
their homeland's climate and growing season, Norwegians settled across the
Northeast and Midwest in large numbers.[38]

Where Norwegians settled, they built ski jumps: in Minnesota, Michigan
and Wisconsin in the early 1880s and '90s, many ski jumps were erected, all
organized by Norwegians and often requiring Norwegian ancestry to join.[39]
The Berlin Mill Ski Club in Berlin, New Hampshire, was the earliest ski club
in the Northeast, founded in 1872. Named after the town's sawmill industry,

Hill preparation on the Nansen Ski Jump, likely 1939: the flags suggest the Olympic Tryouts and FIS World Championship. *Warren Chivers Archive.*

the club held winter carnivals and was renamed Skiklubben Fridtjof Nansen after the Norwegian skier. Later, the name was shortened to the Nansen Ski Club. Berlin's eighty-meter ski jump became the largest hill in the East, enabling it to hold the 1939 Olympic Jumping Team Tryouts and the 1940 U.S. National Championships.[40]

Lake Placid in Upstate New York became a ski jumping hub in the early 1900s, aided by the easily accessible New York Central Railway system. The Lake Placid Club, a resort established in 1895, began ordering skis from Norway in 1904 to promote winter activities for its guests, and in 1921, the club built several ski jumps. Lake Placid hosted the first Eastern Championship in 1924 and the first Winter Olympic Games held in the United States in 1932.[41]

Many Norwegians settled in New York City starting in the mid-1800s. A 1971 *New York Times* article stated that Norwegians

> *began settling in Brooklyn 150 years ago, largely in the Red Hook section, and then they moved gradually until about 75 years ago, when they took hold in Bay Ridge. There are still 30,000 Norwegians in Bay Ridge, with the building trades the predominant occupation….As one resident put it: "Bay Ridge is the fourth largest city of Norway. First is Oslo, second is Bergen, third is Stavanger—and fourth is Bay Ridge."*[42]

Because of this concentration of Norwegians in the New York metropolitan area, ski jumping clubs and nine jumping hills sprouted up in the area,[43] including the Norway Ski Club of Westchester County, the Norwegian-American Ski Club and the Norsemen Ski Club of Brooklyn.[44] There was even a ski jump towering ninety feet high in White Plains, New York, built by a group of Norwegians in 1927. During the building process, a strong wind destroyed it, and members of the community volunteered to help rebuild the jump in time for its first competition. A *New York Times* article recounted that with five thousand spectators watching, "Thirty jumpers showed up, and most were hesitant because in the rush to rebuild, the workers had not removed all the old stumps and boulders in the run-out. As an expedient, they marked them with red flags and assumed the jumpers would be able to ski around them after they landed."[45] About an hour north of New York City, Bear Mountain's forty-five-meter hill was the largest of its kind in the New York City area and an important training jump for the Northeast through the 1980s, sometimes attracting a crowd of thirty-five thousand.[46]

Hill preparation on the White Plains ski jump, 1927. *Warren Chivers Archive.*

The predominance of ski jumping in the New York City area was matched by the enthusiasm for the sport in the state of New Hampshire. Ski jumping clubs were established throughout the state, such as the Winnipesaukee Ski Club in 1918[47] and the Dartmouth Outing Club in 1922 in Hanover, and in the 1930s, jumps were built in Lebanon and Gilford. Many more jumps were built over the next decades in New

Hampshire. In Vermont, the Brattleboro Outing Club was established for ski jumping in 1922. Brattleboro hosted State, New England and National Championships, and starting in 1924, it held an annual "Ski Jump Ball" after the event, with Paul Whiteman's Leviathan Orchestra playing the first year.[48] To the north, the Poland Spring resort in Maine offered ski jumping to its guests starting in 1916, and in the 1920s and '30s jumps were built in Rumford, Augusta, Portland and Bethel, Maine.[49]

Massachusetts and Connecticut were also home to numerous ski jumps. In Salisbury, Connecticut, the Salisbury Outing Club was founded in 1926 by two Norwegian brothers, John Olaf and Magnus Satre, who immigrated from Norway in 1924. In the *New York Times*,

> *Local legend says that in 1926, John Satre, a Norwegian who immigrated to the area, climbed to the top of a barn that still stands in town. The local mountains, the highest in the state, had reminded him of home. From the peak of the barn's roof, Satre put on his skis and flew down the shingles on one side. He landed 30 feet away and lived to tell about it. More important, so did the 200 townsfolk who watched.*[50]

The Salisbury Outing Club, now the Salisbury Winter Sports Association, held its first tournament in 1927, and in 1929, the club hosted the first Connecticut Championships, followed by the Eastern Regionals of the Olympic Trials in 1931 in front of a crowd of eight thousand.[51] The towns of Winsted,[52] Norfolk[53] and Sharon,[54] Connecticut, also held ski jumps. In Massachusetts, jumps were built at the Berkshire School as well as in Williamstown for Williams College students and Pittsfield.[55] There was also a fifty-meter jump in Ayer, a thirty-meter in Quincy, a forty-meter in Bolton, Massachusetts,[56] and a jump in Greenfield that attracted "more than 2,000 spectators to a single event during the height of competition."[57]

Ski jumping and skiing in the Northeast gained popularity with the organization of college ski clubs, "ski trains" or "snow trains" and winter carnivals in the early 1900s, which brought the spectacular snow sports to cities and towns and inspired excitement for winter among the American public. Ski jumping was even featured as a spectacle as much as a sport in the circus acts of Barnum and Bailey in 1909; the most notable ski jumper in the act was Carl Howelson, who emigrated from Norway in 1905 and became known as the "Flying Norseman."[58] In 1916, the *New York Times* reported: "Dartmouth's sixth annual Winter carnival…reached its full swing this afternoon with a Varsity hockey match, ski-joring, skiing, snowshoe

A 1937 poster for a jumping competition in Norfolk. *The Norfolk Historical Society.*

races, and an exhibition of ski jumping before a record breaking crowd assembled from all parts of the United States and Canada."[59] Ski trains transported new winter sports enthusiasts via railroad to northern mountain towns for weekend trips.[60] A 1938 *New York Times* announced: "250 on Special Ski Train: The first de luxe 'snow train' of the season, the Saks Fifth Avenue Laurentian-Quebec Special, left last night from the Grand Central Terminal with a capacity party of 250 skiers aboard."[61] Skiing was increasingly a social activity, a place to meet people and a fun weekend activity for those who could afford it. Founder of the New England Lost Ski Areas Project Jeremy Davis adds that "the trains also were portable resorts in a way, often acting as a base lodge with food service, restrooms and a space to warm up. They also provided for much social interaction, often hosting parties, music, dancing and meals."[62]

Skiing was becoming a part of New England winter culture. In the 1930s, ski jumps were erected for winter ski shows in Madison Square Garden in New York City, the Boston Garden and for the New York World's Fair, where jumpers showed off their skills in front of huge crowds, introducing city dwellers to the excitement of winter sports.[63] A 1936 *New York Times* article announced the upcoming show in Madison Square Garden: "This carnival, probably the most comprehensive ever attempted in New York, will find the Garden transformed. An Alpine setting—snow and scenery reminiscent of the Tyrol as well as the popular snow spots of New York State and New England, will be the background….Ski-jumping, the greatest spectacle of all, will hold the Garden's spotlight."[64]

In the 1930s and '40s, skiing in the United States exploded in popularity.[65] It was inexpensive, and many small towns in the Northeast established their own ski hill operations, making the sport accessible to a large swath of the population. In 1936, a ticket to ski at Stowe in Vermont was one dollar,[66] and with the first rope tow in Woodstock, Vermont, in 1934,[67] the public could ski without having to hike back up to the top of the hill for another run. As ski journalist and historian Morten Lund points out, "Many of the ropes were conveniently situated, close to towns and cities, making entry into the sport easy in every sense. The state of Maine eventually put up over a hundred rope tows."[68] Where there were ski areas, there were often ski jumps, too.

According to Larry Stone, ski jumping wasn't just a sport for the elite. Stone, former coach of the Men's and Women's U.S. Ski Jumping Teams and longtime coach at Lake Placid, recalls: "All these blue collar worker guys had a sport to go to in the winter. It was clubs against other clubs; it was a really neat part of country living."[69] Stone grew up skiing and jumping and said that jumpers and volunteers from the community worked together on the hills to get them ready for practice; kids jumped after school with their friends at their local hills. As he noted of his hometown, Salisbury, Connecticut,

> *"When I grew up in the '50s here,"…"there were eight, maybe nine jumps in town. We all even had them in our backyards. We'd make them on little hillsides. And you just grew up here doing it like kids play baseball anywhere else." Stone and his neighbors competed against kids from places like Norfolk, Bear Mountain, White Plains and Rosendale, N.Y. Back in the 1950s, ski jumping was a normal part of small town culture in New England. But, somewhere along the way, that culture was lost. "All those towns that I was talking about, they don't have jumps anymore," Stone said. "Used to be dozens of them and now there's just a handful."[70]*

Though a booming American sport through the middle of the twentieth century, ski jumping's popularity began to wane. A 1982 *New York Times* article noted that "jumpers…appear to be heading for the endangered species list of sports, going the way of gladiators and jousting knights."[71] Today, only a handful of clubs remain active. Moreover, jumping hills are hard work to keep snow-covered and maintained throughout the winter for training; most ski jumping programs rely on a group of skilled and dedicated volunteers to keep the sport going.

Women's ski jumping, an entire subject in its own right, is only briefly mentioned here. For much of the twentieth century, ski jumping was a male-dominated sport. Though women have jumped since the 1860s, the sport excluded women from taking part in high-level competitions until recent decades.

In 1863, Norwegian Ingrid Olsdatter Vestby was the first recorded female to compete in ski jumping,[72] and in 1896, the first unofficial national competition for women was organized by the Norwegian Asker Ski Club, called the Landesrennet for Damer, in which twenty women took part. Known as the "Floating Baroness," Paula Von Lamberg, an Austrian baroness, competed with men in ski jumping competitions around 1911.[73]

Women persisted in ski jumping internationally throughout the twentieth century, finally fighting their way to the front and demanding equality in the sport in the twenty-first century. After a long fight for inclusion, women were finally allowed to compete in the Winter Olympic Games in 2014, but the fight for full inclusion at the highest levels of the sport continues.

During the 2018–19 winter season, there were fewer than one thousand jumpers in the United States and fewer than two hundred ski jumpers in the Northeast.[74] Ski jumping in the Northeast endured significant challenges to its survival in the 1970s and '80s; today, some clubs and jumping programs struggle to stay afloat, yet there is a certain draw to ski jumping in the Northeast that can gather communities together to keep kids jumping.

3

A DWINDLING AMERICAN SPORT

Though a booming American sport through the 1950s and '60s, ski jumping began a decline in the 1970s and 1980s that was marked by a drop in participation, the deterioration of jumping facilities and, in many cases, the abandoning of ski jumps altogether. There were several reasons for this trend. First, fewer Scandinavians were immigrating to the United States, and Scandinavian communities in the Northeast that were once ski jumping's driving force were dissipating. Second, a viral video clip made ski jumping famous in 1970 for one terrible crash, increasing public perceptions that the sport was dangerous. Third, in 1981, the National Collegiate Athletic Association voted to drop ski jumping as a college sport, a decision that was felt in every corner of the U.S. ski jumping community. The subsequent move away from the traditional four-event skiing discipline known as skimeister further diminished the sport. Skiers no longer competed in ski jumping together with cross-country skiing, slalom skiing and giant slalom skiing, and while the more widely practiced sports of cross-country and alpine skiing took off, ski jumping was left behind. These challenges caused the pool of jumpers, coaches, officials and volunteers to shrink, leading to the collapse of many ski jumps throughout the Northeast.

Norwegian immigration and its influence on ski jumping helped carry the sport through the mid-twentieth century, but with fewer Norwegians immigrating to the United States in the 1970s and 1980s, locally run ski jumps began to suffer. From 1825 until 1924, roughly 800,000 Norwegians settled in the States.[75] The 1924 Immigration Act aimed to stop immigration from parts of southern and eastern Europe, but it also slowed Norwegian immigration to the United States.[76] Norwegian yearly immigration dropped further in 1970 to under 4,000 per year, a number that continued to decrease: in 2016, only 93 Norwegians became U.S. citizens.[77]

Ski jumping in America followed the rise and fall of Scandinavian immigration, as a 1982 *New York Times* article commented: "Scandinavian immigrants brought the sport to this country in the late 1800's. Today there are pockets of ski-jumping activity where they settled."[78] At one point, over two hundred ski jumps existed in the northeastern United States.[79] Mark Levasseur, born in 1960 in Worcester, Massachusetts, remembers Norwegian Americans, including: "Sig Evenson, who came over (from Norway) in his 40s and settled about 10 miles south of Bear Mountain. They would work on the hill, they would coach, they judged, they would do anything and everything."[80] Erling Heistad, a second-generation Norwegian American born in 1939, grew up in Lebanon, New Hampshire. His father, also Erling, emigrated at age fifteen from Norway in 1912 with his younger sister and introduced ski jumping to Lebanon in 1923. Heistad recalled that his father

> *coached and was interested in jumps, so he built eight of them....Well, his write up in the National Ski Hall of Fame says seven jumps in Lebanon, but I know of eight. His goal was that every neighborhood should have a jump that the kids would be responsible for. You had your own jump, your own place that you took care of, and you went and you cut the brush, and you cut the grass and you packed it out and you maintained your place.*[81]

In the Brooklyn-based ski jumping community, Art Tokle was born in 1949 into a family notorious for its ski jumpers: Art's father, a two-time Olympian and former U.S. head coach, was one of five brothers, all ski jumpers, who came to the United States from Norway in the 1920s and '30s. The Tokle family settled in Brooklyn, New York. Tokle confirmed that "there was a big Norwegian community in the Bay Ridge section, and there were a lot of jumpers that came out of that part of Brooklyn."[82] Larry Stone remembered ski jumping's heyday as well: "There were jumps all over the East—there was a place in New York State called Rosendale; there was another place just north of Bear Mountain called Salisbury Mills; there were all kinds of hills, all over the place…and most of (the clubs) were Norwegian, or had that kind of heritage or had been introduced to it."[83]

Slowly, however, interest in maintaining many of these Norwegian-built neighborhood ski jumps collapsed. Ski jumping Olympian Walter

Erling Heistad, circa 1930. *Courtesy of Erling Heistad.*

Malmquist (1980), who was born in 1956 and grew up in Thetford, Vermont, remembered seeing dormant ski jumps in many Vermont towns, including Barre, Montpelier, Underhill and Middlebury in the late 1960s: "I would see these sights where ski jumps had gone dormant because communities made up of Scandinavians, the people that brought the sport from Europe with them, and the interest of those families did not survive from generation to generation, except in some communities."[84] By the '70s and '80s, ski jumping in the metropolitan area was also running on fumes. Levasseur recalled, "My favorite place to ski jump was Bear Mountain, New York. It was a bunch of Norwegians who started it, and it was a group of Norwegians who were there organizing it, and when they all died off, the whole thing crumbled. So we don't have that—that generation is gone. Ski jumping was booming here in the East because of the Norwegians."[85] The Bear Mountain ski jump, once in the running to be used in the 1932 Winter Olympics, went dormant in 1990: the natural inrun and landing hill are now overgrown.[86]

Similarly, in New Hampshire, many of those jumps Heistad's father built, along with others in the state, fell out of use in the 1970s and '80s. Heistad described one overgrown and dormant jump: "There was a cribbed up log takeoff. The logs have now settled into the ground, but you can still take a brush scythe and you could still go ahead and mow that out and jump it if you wanted to…most of the jumps when they get disused and not maintained anymore, they go back to mother nature."[87]

Ironically, it was television, the medium that had brought ski jumping to the general public, that helped hasten the decline of its popularity. In the 1970 Oberstdorf World Cup Ski Jumping Championships in West Germany, Slovenian Vinko Bogataj fell spectacularly while skiing down the inrun of the jump, tumbling off the high takeoff and down the side of the slope, scattering hill markers and spectators. The crash was picked up by ABC and played every Saturday afternoon as the opening to ABC's *Wide World of Sports* for decades. In the introduction, host Jim McKay would dramatically announce, "Spanning the globe to bring you the constant variety of sport…the thrill of victory…and the agony of defeat [cue the crash]…the human drama of athletic competition.…This is ABC's Wide World of Sports!"[88] For many, watching ABC's *Wide World of Sports* was a Saturday afternoon tradition, as sports writer Dave Miller remembered: "Growing up in the 60s, sports were an important part of my life.…Often, the entire day was consumed with things like baseball, football, badminton, or even croquet. Except on Saturdays at 3:30. That's when we all headed inside for a little break to watch 'The Wide World of Sports.'"[89]

Bogataj's failed ski jump attempt and ski jumping itself likely came to epitomize "the agony of defeat" for many Americans. Malmquist recalled the video's effect on ski jumping: "It puts salt in a wound, definitely. You don't see that many ski jumps that end up in a fall, but you take the worst imaginable situation and you televise that on a weekly basis, to people who

Bear Mountain, 1965. *Courtesy of Sammlung F.H. and skisprungschanzen.com.*

are watching other sports.…It's just…it's not a representation of our sport. And it clearly prevents some people from considering trying it out."[90]

Heistad noted, "I think the 'Wide World of Sports' did more to bring jumping into the doldrums than anything else—that one clip showed over and over again…an awful lot of parents became convinced that their kid was never going to get anywhere near a ski jump after seeing that."[91] Ski jumper and coach in Andover, New Hampshire Chris Jones, born in 1986 and a Sutton, New Hampshire native, noted that "ABC's 'Wide World of Sports' 'The Agony of Defeat' was on people's TV every single weekend, so they opened the TV program and got to watch the ski jumper absolutely eat shit on the beginning of the program.…So nobody wants to go and try that and be like, 'oh yeah, that's a safe thing.'"[92]

When the National Collegiate Athletic Association (NCAA) dropped ski jumping as a sanctioned college sport in 1981, ski jumping in the United States further deteriorated. That year, the NCAA Skiing Committee, which was made up of five people—an athletic director and four ski coaches—voted unanimously to drop ski jumping from its list of sanctioned college sports.[93] The people I interviewed agreed that this decision alone did more damage to ski jumping across the country than any other event. Stone said:

> *When the college thing happened, that put everything back four very important years, so that if you hadn't showed that you could make it to a pretty high level and start skiing internationally by the time you were out of high school, you were shit out of luck, or else you had to self finance, or put off college, or all these other factors…so that just cut the whole backbone out of it.…It cut back on officials and coaches, on numbers of people jumping at a high level until later in life, and that really was a huge factor.*[94]

Ski jumping had been a flourishing college sport since 1910, when Dartmouth College and McGill University held their first ski jumping meet. In New England, Tokle recalled, "Almost every major college had a ski jumping team. Even Ted Kennedy jumped at Harvard University."[95]

Heistad recalled the prevalence of college jumping in the 1950s at Lebanon Outing Club:

> *I remember coming back one day and my father was going down this list, and he counted them up and he says, "Twenty-one!" and I said, "Of what?" He said, "Twenty-one colleges and schools have been training here this weekend."…Yeah, try to find twenty-one schools in New England that have ski jumpers now. You know, they're just not there. But it used to be very busy. That was the early '50s. College jumping was a big deal.*[96]

Harvard, Yale, Bowdoin, Middlebury, Dartmouth, Colgate, Cornell and Bates Colleges, to name a few, all had ski jumping teams.[97] Levasseur remembered,

> *In the early '70s at Salisbury, Connecticut, there were close to one hundred jumpers, and you had to make the top sixty to jump on Sunday. That was because there was college jumping.…So if you had ten schools and they each sent four or five jumpers, there were forty or fifty college kids. When they ended college jumping, it did quite a lot of damage to ski jumping in the East, because there was no reason for a kid to continue.*[98]

When colleges stopped offering ski jumping, it resulted in a chain of events that had negative effects on the sport. High school jumping programs in all states except for New Hampshire ceased to exist.[99] A 2012 *New York Times* article commented on the issue: "A frustration for (high school) participants is that there is no next logical step from this level of competition."[100] Where once there was an incentive for towns to support their local ski jump because it meant supporting local kids in a sport they could continue through college and beyond, now there was no realistic future for young aspiring jumpers. Malmquist recalled, "Thinking about Barre, Vermont, a community of granite workers and woodworkers, it was a blue-collar community.…Many local programs, which included high school populations as well as elementary school populations, didn't see where opportunities to ski jump would take their young people."[101]

Considering the effect the NCAA's decision had on ski jumping, Malmquist noted, "I think what that should say to people is that not only was it important for NCAA to maintain its programs so that clubs had a reason to support ski jumping in their local communities, but it also provided athletes with an arena that they could advance themselves

An early jump at the Snow Bowl, known at the time as the Cold Creek Valley Ski Hill, 1941. *St. Lawrence University, Special Collections, Owen D. Young Library.*

without skiing at an international level."[102] Without this opportunity to ski jump at a college level, an entire section of the developmental opportunities for ski jumpers in the United States disappeared. Jones noted that eliminating college jumping "kind of wiped out your mid-tier. You've got your kids that are coming through high school…and then from there they could go and compete in the college circuit.…When you pull the rug out from underneath that, now you're trying to get kids from high school to the National Team. Those four years make a huge difference."[103] In Malmquist's words,

Colleges can and did provide programs that coached developing athletes as well as elite athletes, and that doesn't exist in the United States anymore. The colleges used to have great coaches. They used to prepare their facilities, and now it's done on a volunteer basis rather than having professionals or clubs at colleges helping to put the hills in shape. Local programs have a much greater burden now, so bless all the volunteers who are working to help ski jumping survive, in advance.[104]

Colleges were increasingly recruiting Norwegian ski jumpers in order to to stay competitive, and the Norwegians usually dominated college events, often bumping Americans out of the running. A 1968 *New York Times* article alluded to this phenomenon: "Hanover, Nh., Feb 10—Per Edward Coucheran, a blond blue-eyed ski jumper from Norway, performed his specialty in the face of a gusty snow storm today and helped his college, Dartmouth, win its own winter carnival."[105] Malmquist laughed, recalling, "One of the reasons I didn't go to UVM was because they were stocked with Norwegians, [which could make it difficult to advance on the team],"[106] and 1984 ski jumping Olympian Jeff Hastings noted, "Most of the coaches were sick of problems with facilities and of trying to get Norwegian recruits so they could be competitive."[107] There were other issues that made college jumping less tenable: the maintenance of ski jumps was labor intensive and expensive, making ski jumping programs at all levels vulnerable to collapse, and the cost of insurance to sanction skiing sports was rising. The NCAA also planned to start sanctioning women's events, and at the time, there were very few female ski jumpers in the United States.[108]

Stone and Heistad think that beyond these factors, there was a group of coaches who did not want to deal with the challenge of keeping their own teams competitive, and they pushed to have college jumping discontinued.[109] In Stone's opinion,

It was the UVM coach, the Middlebury coach and the Colorado coach.... They kinda all got together and said, "You know, we feel at a big disadvantage without a facility, and we don't want to build a facility…" Basically it was just a political hatchet job…a few of the major college coaches got together and said, "Let's just get rid of jumping," and one of the arguments they used was, "Well, we basically all bring Euros over, anyway, so it really isn't much of a help to us, and we'll just get rid of that."…A lot of the coaches didn't want to do that—it was just sort of pushed through by a little nucleus of guys. I mean guys my age, we still hold it against those guys. If you ever see them, you just have to bite your tongues and not go over and yell at them.[110]

From 1981 through 1993, Dartmouth College alone resisted closing its ski jump. In the 1990s, however, the jump was finally shut down for good and demolished, as sportswriter Dennis Gildea lamented:

Shortly after the last of the snow from the March blizzard of 1993 melted in northern New England, the wrecking crew moved onto the Dartmouth College golf course in Hanover, New Hampshire, and began dismantling the ski jumping tower. Within the small subculture of North American ski jumpers, the demise of the Dartmouth jump was big and sad news…. Erected in 1921 and the oldest campus jump in the United States, [it] was…a historical landmark, a symbol of a time when college athletics were becoming organized, formalized, and popularized.[111]

An additional consequence of the NCAA's decision was the loss of the skimeister discipline and the ensuing separation of ski jumping from cross-country and alpine skiing. Until the 1980s, NCAA ski jumping events were often organized as skimeister competitions, in which a ski jumper competed in four skiing events: ski jumping, cross-country, slalom and giant slalom. The winner of a skimeister meet was the one skier who performed the best in all four events,[112] earning skimeister honor for their college or university.[113] This combined event was likely a holdover from an older tradition that was in practice until the 1930s: that *all* ski jumpers were required to compete in both cross-country skiing and jumping any time they entered a competition.[114]

Skimeister, however, was not just for college jumpers; many local clubs organized skimeister meets as well. Lebanon Outing Club in New Hampshire has hosted a yearly skimeister competition for decades. The *Lebanon Times* announced, "The annual Mud Meet crowns the 'Skimeister of Lebanon and the World' with awards in ski jumping, Nordic skiing, and downhill racing."[115] Heistad remembered the four-event discipline as the standard: "If you were a skier, you skied everything, and that meant when we finished cross-country practice, we'd go over and jump the twenty. There wasn't as much specialization, so I got started back in the '40s as a wee tyke, and coming up through the '50s, all of our meets were four events; we never went to a meet without skiing four events."[116] Malmquist recalled learning to ski in the 1950s and '60s: "Back then, you learned to walk on skis before you learned to slide on skis, and when you could turn, then you went to jumping. So you learned left and right skills and powerful skills from alpine skiing. You acquired endurance from cross-country, and it all culminated in jumping."[117]

When asked why there were so many more ski jumpers in the 1950s and '60s, Malmquist responded, "I attribute that to the fact that the skimeister discipline was a very popular event back in the '50s and '60s."[118] The fall of the skimeister hurt the sport. As skiers were forced to choose between skiing disciplines, many chose alpine and cross-country skiing over jumping, both of which were growing in popularity at the time: a 1976 article in the *Chicago Tribune* announced cross-country skiing as the "fastest growing sport in North America, according to the Ski Touring Council of Troy, Vt…Suddenly this outdoor diversion ranks in rising popularity right up there with tennis."[119]

As cross-country and alpine skiing grew, Malmquist recalled, "Ski jumping was on its own. Cross country grew as ski jumping unfortunately was going through a slump, a major slump."[120] After the NCAA dropped ski jumping as a college sport, local and high school jumping programs suffered. Malmquist noted,

The cascading effects (of the NCAA's decision) soon significantly reduced the number of facilities with ski jump programs as well as the number of junior ski jumpers in the United States….which in turn led to the USSA and US Ski Team dropping ski jumping from their programs, while local and regional cross country programs, in their own best interests, grew more and more independent from ski jumping.[121]

With less visibility due to the separation of these sports, ski jumping suffered from lower attendance and less access to resources and volunteers. Because of a narrowing pool of volunteers, communities that were too distanced from their Norwegian roots, local programs' limited financial resources and the growing competition with other sports, some ski jumping facilities suffered. By 1977, the wooden tower of the K65 ski jump in Salisbury, which rose fifty feet above the ground, was starting to rot. Walter Malmquist remembered a Norwegian Dartmouth College teammate, Christian Berggrav, falling through the floor at the top of the tower while practicing "imitation" takeoffs before his turn to jump: "I mentioned to Christian—'This wood is pretty tender. I don't think we want to be jumping around up here.'" Luckily, when Christian fell through the planking, he caught himself by his elbows, and after dangling above the fifty-foot drop to the ground, Malmquist was able to hoist him back up to safety:

> *He had old Splitken skis. As I was grabbing him, I could see his skis floating down in the air like a feather, we were so high up, they floated back and forth, going down in the air until they hit the ground....If he had not caught those 2x4s with his elbows sticking out, he wouldn't be with us anymore. I think that that was probably the most exciting thing that happened that day.*[122]

The rest of the day was business as usual, Malmquist remembers. Christian collected his skis and hiked back up to take his jump, and Malmquist set a new hill record that day. Carey Fiertz, a director at Salisbury Winter Sports Association, had another story about the old ski jump tower: he once "met some guys who said that they had been involved when the poles (for the tower) were put in—they actually operated the pole digging device, and they said they were sure they didn't put them in deep enough....I still shudder when I look at pictures of the old tower."[123]

I interviewed my father, Mark Picton, who recalled the ski jumping program in Salisbury, Connecticut, when I first started jumping in 1999: "There was a real mix of equipment,"[124] he recalled, which, he said, included wooden antique jumping skis from the 1930s and '40s that no one used, skis from the '60s and '70s that jumpers who were just starting out used and a smaller collection of newer jumping skis, used by more advanced jumpers, all of which were hand-me-downs from other clubs or past jumpers.[125] My father described finding equipment for me and other jumpers in the ski shed:

> *It was—you go into the ski shed and find something that's the right length for you, and you see if the bindings are working. If they're not, someone will take out a screwdriver and switch something around, and, you know, borrow a binding part from some other ski, and pretty soon this kid is equipped and ready to fly down the hill....It was cobbled together, but there was nothing wrong with that.*[126]

Despite all the difficulties the ski jumping community has faced, ski jumping persists, and it continues to be a viable sport to this day. Even though college jumping is no longer an option in the United States, American ski jumpers still find their way to the highest levels of the sport.

Those committed to ski jumping in the twenty-first century continue to seek out ways to reestablish bonds between jumping clubs and their communities while enabling young jumpers to achieve their goals in the sport. Perhaps it is the small-scale aspect of ski jumping programs that motivates volunteers to continue, or perhaps it is the sense of togetherness and solidarity that comes from being involved in a neighborhood-fed sport that keeps ski jumping programs alive, but one thing is certain: the ski jumping community is resilient.

4

THE POWER OF COMMUNITY

Ski Jumping's Success in the Northeast

Despite its decline in the second half of the twentieth century, ski jumping continues to have a small but strong community and following in the twenty-first century. Several factors contribute to this. First, ski jumping is an Olympic event and has been since the Winter Games began; this provides a consistent goal for aspiring young jumpers. Second, women's ski jumping has gained a great deal of traction in recent decades; after a long and ongoing battle for women's inclusion at the highest levels of the sport, women were finally allowed to compete in the Olympics in 2014, marking a huge step toward gender equality in ski jumping. Third, a unique sense of tradition in the northeastern United States surrounds the sport, and local communities keep it going. Fourth, strong communities of volunteers still run various ski jumping clubs around the East; in fact, many jumping events and programs simply could not stay alive without them.

The Winter Olympics every four years contributes to a sense of stability in the sport and is a goal for many ski jumpers. Ski jumping was one of the few original Winter Olympic sports, included in 1924 in the first Winter Olympic Games in Chamonix, France.[127] Lake Placid, New York, hosted the 1932 Winter Games and again in 1980, making it the only site that has hosted the Winter Games in the eastern United States.[128] A February 1932 *Chicago Daily Tribune* article announced: "The 1932 Olympic Games… will begin at 10 a.m. tomorrow in the snowy village of Lake Placid, in the Adirondack Mountains of New York.…The climax, of course, will be the ski jumps and the bob races next week."[129] The "snowy village of Lake Placid" had actually been suffering through unseasonably mild weather leading up to the Games, as the *Washington Post* observed that January:

> *All day long rain fell on a rugged countryside that has been stripped clean of snow and ice. Anywhere else the mildness of spring and temperatures above 50 degrees might be welcomed but here it strikes straight at the heart of a community that for a solid year has bent every activity toward preparation for the international competitions starting February 4 and continuing through February 13. Skiers of Norway, Japan and Sweden, eager for practice, can't find enough snow to make a snowball. In the hotels today faces brightened at the posting of the official report: "Rain, changing to light snow. Much colder tonight. Saturday snow. Clearing by night. Drop in temperature. Fair. Near zero Sunday."* [130]

Snow fell just in time for the Games to be held, but the United States won no ski jumping medals that year. In fact, Americans have won very few Olympic medals in ski jumping or Nordic combined since the first Olympic Games, but a few victories stand out.

In the very first Olympics in Chamonix, Norwegian-born American Anders Haugen won the Bronze Medal. To date, Haugen is the only American to win an Olympic medal in "Special Jumping"—the sport of

Birger Ruud during the 1932 Olympic Games in Lake Placid. *Warren Chivers Archive.*

ski jumping without the inclusion of a cross-country skiing race.[131] The next medals won by Americans were more than eight decades later in the 2010 Vancouver Olympic Games when the United States won a staggering four medals in Nordic combined—an event that combines points from ski jumping and cross-country skiing. These were the first medals ever won by Americans in Nordic combined. Johnny Spillane won the Silver Medal on the K90 meter hill; on the K120 meter hill, Bill Demong won Gold and Johnny Spillane won Silver; and in the team event, the United States won Silver.[132] For the United States, winning in Nordic events has been an uphill battle. The *New York Times* noted that "Nordic combined has been dominated by countries—like Norway, Finland and Germany—where cross-country skiing and ski jumping are popular."[133] While the list of medals won by Americans in ski jumping and Nordic combined is short, these ski jumpers provided young American jumpers with role models. Until the twenty-first century, however, ski jumping at an elite level excluded women from participation.

In 2011, the International Olympic Committee (IOC) announced that ski jumping, the only sport in the Winter or Summer Olympics that did not include both men and women, would finally include women in the 2014 Winter Olympic Games in Sochi, Russia. This followed a years-long struggle for women's inclusion, organized by a group of female ski jumpers from around the world.[134] One of the main leaders of the group was American Lindsey Van, the winner of the first ever women's ski jumping World Championships, held in 2009 in Liberec, Czech Republic.[135] Van commented that "I guess since you're the first and only World Champion in your sport, then you're the go-to person all of a sudden. That's a whole new role; it's not something you ever pick, but you're the spokesperson for the sport. That's *your* job."[136]

Lindsey Van, 2009.
Wikimedia Commons.

Prior to the 2011 decision, ski jumping had very little visibility aside from the Olympics.[137] In 2004, several years before women were allowed in the Olympics, four women participated in "ski flying" for the first time: ski jumping that occurs on much larger hills than those in the Olympics.[138] Despite members of the International Ski Federation (FIS) attempting to block the opportunity for the women, supposedly due to safety concerns,

Van was one of four women who went ski flying that day in front of a huge crowd. The women were only allowed to jump in the practice before the men's meet,[139] but Van's coach, Larry Stone, remembered, "I think half of that crowd was there to see the women ski fly.…At the end of the (men's) meet, this old guy who was the head of the FIS jumping committee at that point, he comes over to me and says 'Well, you did it today, but the girls will never ski fly again.' And that was true—that was 2004, and I don't think the girls have flown since."[140]

The policy of excluding women continued in 2002 and in the 2006 Torino Winter Games when the IOC added only one sport to the events, which was ski cross.[141] In 2008, Van along with teammates Jessica Jerome and Karla Keck and twelve other female jumpers from five countries sued the Vancouver Organizing Committee for the right to take part in the 2010 Vancouver Olympic Games.[142] As a result, the British Columbia Supreme Court ruled that the IOC was guilty of gender discrimination in barring women ski jumpers from competing in the Olympics but did not take the next step to force the IOC or the Vancouver Organizing Committee to change its plans for the 2010 Games, so female ski jumpers were again stuck watching from the sidelines.[143] After that court session, a distraught Van spoke to the reporters:

> *I thought that they would go the other way.…It just makes it seem like discrimination is okay in Canada. Kind of like, the Canadian court system is a little bit weak, if they can't even stand up to the IOC and hold by Canadian law. It's like (the IOC) can just come in here and do whatever they want, because they're a private entity, ruled by nobody. So they can go wherever, do whatever.…That's scary!*[144]

The IOC contended that there were not enough women at an elite level of the sport to make it a viable event.[145] The numbers, however, indicated the opposite. In 2006, there were 83 female ski jumpers from 14 countries jumping at an elite level, which was more than luge, skeleton, bobsled, snowboard cross or ski cross could boast of their female elite competitors,[146] and by 2009, Canadian ski jumper Katie Willis said that there were "more than 160 elite women ski jumpers from 18 nations who compete internationally."[147] Furthermore, according to a *New York Times* article, critics of the IOC's decision "charged that the exclusion was based on outdated ideas about the abilities of female athletes, made all the more puzzling by the fact that traditionally male Olympic sports like wrestling and boxing had recently welcomed women."[148] In particular, Gian-Franco Kasper, president of the FIS, was quoted on National Public Radio in 2005 as saying, "Don't forget, it's like jumping down from, let's say, about two meters on the ground about a thousand times a year, which seems not to be appropriate for ladies from a medical point of view."[149] Larry Stone added:

> *There's nothing as daring as a young guy or girl on a ski jump. But there's nothing as stodgy and old fashioned and conservative as the old ski jumpers. So the old guys that were running FIS, basically they were just digging their heels in because the unspoken fear that I think was fueling the resistance of FIS to the women's ski jumping movement, was that they were scared to death that a woman would set the world record in ski flying, and they couldn't handle it.*[150]

The women kept pushing for inclusion, however, and finally triumphed, gaining a spot in the 2014 Olympic Games. Critics of female inclusion in the sport continued even as the Sochi Games began: the men's ski jumping coach for Russia, Alexander Arefyev, commented, "It's a pretty difficult sport with a high risk of injury. If a man gets a serious injury it's still not fatal, but for women it could end much more seriously. Women have another purpose—to have children, to do housework, to create hearth and home."[151]

The joint collaboration of women around the world to promote women's ski jumping was part of its reason for success: Jessica Jerome commented on this sense of camaraderie: "When a new girl wins, even if she's not American, we think that's awesome. If she's getting better, then her teammates are getting better. Then we're all going to get more competitive, and the whole level of the sport gets better."[152] After Van won the first women's World Championship, ski jumper Daniela Iraschko from Austria commented, "I think it was good for women's ski jumping, and I congratulate Lindsey for her gold medal."[153] During the Sochi Games, Van commented, "Being here is history. I want more people to see that women can ski jump. It's taken 90 years for us to get here."[154] This achievement of gaining Olympic status for the sport for women has gone a long way to encourage young girls to try: they can now set real goals of following in the footsteps of female Olympians like Lindsey Van.

Another factor that keeps ski jumping viable is the strong sense of tradition surrounding the sport and ski jumping events and the wish to preserve and continue that tradition. Some ski jumping clubs rely on their once-a-year jumping event to raise money to keep their club going another year. Tickets are sold, along with food, beer, cowbells, hats and T-shirts. The atmosphere at larger ski jumping events can be carnival-like; there are often bonfires, food and beer tents, children and dogs running around and snowball fights. Onlookers ring cowbells instead of clapping their gloved hands when a jumper comes down the hill.[155]

The special atmosphere found at ski jumping events has a way of cultivating fans that choose to make standing out in the cold and watching ski jumping a yearly tradition. A 2010 *New York Times* article noted that the scene surrounding a jumping event almost won out over the actual jumping spectacle itself: "There were certainly no 'agony of defeat' moments of someone cart-wheeling off the ramp….Children nap and fans clang cowbells as daredevils fly….Still, in some ways, ski jumping is comfortably delightful. People jump. Fans cheer….Some things never change."[156]

It is precisely this element of tradition that brings crowds each year to the ski jump in Brattleboro, Vermont, where thousands gather for the annual competition on Harris Hill.[157] For a sport that takes place in the dead of winter, it is remarkable that this event frequently draws so many: in 1972, the *New York Times* noted the "frostbitten crowd of 4,000."[158] Since 1922, Brattleboro has held onto a ski jumping tradition that not only attracts large crowds but also forms a festival-like scene that has made it a tradition worth continuing. As the *Brattleboro Reformer* recalled, "On February 4, 1922 the first Vermont State Championship Ski Jump was held at the Cedar Street jump. About 3,000 spectators saw John Carleton of Dartmouth Outing Club leap 150 feet on his first try….The hill featured a 340-foot toboggan slide, as well as a 60-meter ski jump, a junior ski jump, and an outdoor fireplace."[159]

The atmosphere is similar in Salisbury, Connecticut. Tradition brings crowds back to Salisbury each year, two weekends prior to Brattleboro's event. Spectators drive from hours away to watch the ski jumping in Salisbury, where "onlookers drink beer, hot cocoa and warm themselves by dueling bonfires,"[160] outdoor writer Katharine Erwin noted. Tucked away in the woods on the outskirts of town, the ski jumps have formed a following because of the tradition that was started years ago. Larry Stone agrees: "'I grew up here. It's a homegrown club with a huge tradition that goes way way back into the '30s.'"[161] This ski jumping event continues to draw in crowds simply because people love the tradition of it. The *Hartford Courant* related that "Jacqui Rice, a math teacher at Housatonic Valley Regional High School…has been coming to watch the ski jumping since she was a kid. 'When I was young, my dad was the starter at the top of

Skiers pack the landing hill of the Brattleboro jump, 1930s. *Warren Chivers Archive.*

the hill,' Rice said. 'As a youngster, I came and collected bibs, that kind of stuff. My mother worked in the snack shack.'"[162] The excitement around Salisbury's big "Jumpfest" weekend revolves around tradition: Mark Picton noted, "In Salisbury, people feel strongly about the jumps because it's a whole community tradition. That's why people come back to coach and help on the hill, because it's a tradition in their lives…not only in the history of the town, but in the history of individual lives."[163] Mat Kiefer, a longtime member of the Salisbury Winter Sports Association Board of Directors, thinks the reason volunteers keep showing up year after year is simply that "everybody is just working so hard to keep a tradition going."[164]

It was also thanks to tradition that Salisbury was able to build a new sixty-five-meter ski jump in 2009. When members of Salisbury Winter Sports Association held a town meeting to discuss whether the club should try to raise $700,000 to replace the rotting and rickety ski jump that was no longer safe to use, Kiefer remembered that

> *300 people showed up. 297 voted for it, felt it was a good idea.…They weren't members of the club, they were just people that lived in town. People*

The brand-new sixty-five-meter hill, Salisbury, Connecticut, 2010. *By Joe Meehan, The Salisbury Association Photo Archive.*

got up and spoke about it.… "It's part of our town heritage, it's such a happy thing, this is something that we think is important to continue on as a tradition."…There was a guy that got up and said, "You guys gotta do this!" Jon and I, when we left, we had tears in our eyes.[165]

Tied into the element of tradition is the importance of volunteers to keep each eastern ski jump alive. In Salisbury, "Every Sunday morning, year-round, a group of volunteers (who refer to themselves as Swamp Yankees) drive down the back road in a picturesque New England setting to meet up and to maintain the jumps. There is no monetary return, just the hope that they will have a great Jumpfest,"[166] Erwin explained. Ski jumps across the East have always been largely volunteer run. There is a strong tradition of volunteers who count on helping out at their local ski jump each winter. In Brattleboro, volunteer coordinator Kathryn Einig noted that "many of the volunteers have been volunteering for longer than I've been recruiting for volunteers. It's true. So when I call them or email them, they write back and say, 'I'm in, I can't wait.'"[167]

Members of the Kiefer family have volunteered at the Salisbury jumps for seventy years. Mat Kiefer's father, George, joined Salisbury Winter Sports Association in 1949: "He got involved in the ski jump as a laborer, a volunteer.…He was the guy that organized the tractors. He would always have a truck full of shovels and rakes and a chainsaw…because you never knew what had to be done. So that's how he started, it was just because it was a local event."[168] Because ski jumping in the East has remained such a small sport over the decades, ski jumping clubs often cannot hire people to work. Picton recalled, "Our club seemed like a local club of dedicated volunteers, and it turned out that most of them go way back with it, and they just continue not out of any obligation, but just because they like the skiing and the associations."[169]

In Salisbury and throughout the East, the weather is also often a huge challenge. Volunteers go to great lengths to make jumping events possible, even in the face of foul weather or a snowless season. It can be a daunting feat to get snow onto a ski jump and to keep it there long enough for a competition to happen. Picton wondered at the immense effort volunteers put in at the ski jumps in Salisbury: "No matter what the conditions they faced, this group of volunteers in Salisbury will put a groomed surface on the jumps and make them ready for safe competition in the face of all kinds of odds, as far as weather goes. I don't know where they get the drive and determination to do that, but they're not going to be deterred by weather or strategic difficulties."[170] Many of the volunteers in Salisbury, at least, came out of a Yankee culture of innovation, in which you made do with what you had. Kiefer described the process of getting snow to and on the ski jumps throughout the years: "Because there was no snowmaking, you had to go find snow in snow drifts on different farms and from snow

Hill preparation on the sixty-five-meter inrun in Salisbury, Connecticut, 1970s. *The Salisbury Association Photo Archive.*

fences along highways."[171] Once snow was collected from parking lots, farms and highways and trucked to the jump, the snow was blown up a pipe onto the ski jump. This method was used in the 1950s and is still used in Salisbury today: at the base of the pipe, a group of volunteers shovels snow and ice chunks into a corn or silage blower, which is a piece of farm

Block ice from Torrington being chopped and blown with a silage blower into a truck and cart, circa 1950. *By Ward Hutchinson, The Salisbury Association Photo Archive.*

equipment run by a tractor. The blower is attached to the vertical pipe that goes fifty feet up to the top of the tower, and the snow is shot straight up the pipe and out onto the inrun of the ski jump. At the top, another group of volunteers is stationed on the inrun, raking and shoveling the blown snow into place to make a smooth inrun for the jumpers.

With the modern snowmaking abilities, the Salisbury jump happens every year now, but Kiefer remembers when the decision to hold the competition had to be left to the last week:

> *You wouldn't know whether to hold a jump until you make a decision the week before, and most particularly, the Monday before. So you would meet on Monday at the drugstore coffee shop. The man in charge of advertising would come, and everybody in charge of hill preparation would come, and you'd all sit down—because the day before, you went to do an inventory on snow banks. Whether it was at Sharon Hospital parking lot, or if it was at some grocery market over in Millerton, or at Berkshire School… then you had to listen to the weatherman and make the decision of whether to hold it or not.[172]*

One July, to raise funds, volunteers in Salisbury put on a summer ski jumping event, again, using the tractor and silage blower to crush lake ice that had been stored in an icehouse through the winter. Kiefer recalls that his father George was involved in the 1955 summer jumping event in Salisbury, where the inrun and landing hill was covered with ice and the outrun was hay: "They worked all night with crushed ice, from an icehouse in Torrington with three or four flatbed trucks. So the big thing was to get the thing going, get it ready....They had a good crowd....Dad said that they worked all night to crush the ice, they had the competition at nine, and the ice was gone by eleven."[173]

Lake Placid also went to great effort to pull off summer ski jumping events. On July 2, 1956, Lake Placid held a summer jump, also largely a volunteer effort. A 1956 *New York Times* reported:

> *Preparing the course will be quite an operation. Fifty tons of ice will arrive by train from Utica tomorrow night and will be trucked to the jumping hill. In past years, the ice has been cut in the winter from nearby lakes, but last winter the snow was too heavy for ice cutting…At 6 A.M. Wednesday a crew of volunteers will be readying the course.…*[They] *expect about 50 to help on the course and more than 100 on the whole project.…Slush would be the expected result of snow in July, but it's no problem here. After the "snow" is laid down on the jump and landing, it is coated with ammonium chloride, which keeps it from melting for twelve to fourteen hours.*[174]

As Heistad notes, "Volunteers, and how you treat your volunteers, will make or break (your ski jumping club). The first thing a volunteer needs to know is that they're wanted, that they're needed, that they're appreciated. Don't ever let a volunteer leave without being thanked."[175]

There is a strong sense of camaraderie present within the ski jumping community, creating an atmosphere that attracts volunteers and spectators who make watching this sport their annual tradition. Ski jumpers cheer each other on. Parents of ski jumpers become close friends. At different meets around the Northeast, jumpers stay with other jumping families. Each weekend, you see the same people over and over again, and this forms a strong bond. This is something that sets the sport apart from others. Women's ski jumping gained traction and made it to the Olympics because women from around the world joined forces to overcome discrimination. Volunteers continue to help out at ski jumps because of this camaraderie. There is a sense of togetherness that sets ski jumping apart from other sports.

1935 Summer Jump on the thirty-five-meter hill, Salisbury, Connecticut. Ole Hegge and Ottar Satre are visible in the judges' tower. *By Gene Mitchell, The Salisbury Association Photo Archive.*

When my ski jumping coach quit in the middle of my jumping career, there was no coach to replace him, and my father recalled that "you were taken on by other clubs and coaches…which is a pretty interesting aspect of ski jumping in New England…that you could still pursue the sport by the grace of six other clubs in New England. The other coaches were always willing to coach whoever was on the hill, practicing or competing."[176] Heistad also commented on this unique aspect of the sport. He compared it to the downhill/alpine racing scene. He recounted how his son's downhill racing skis were once tampered with by another racer so that he fell during a race:

> *Now, can you picture that happening to a jumping ski? No. Very, very different. What makes that difference? Probably all sorts of things, but the difference is there, and something that parents should appreciate: that their kids are going to be taken care of… I think that our working together and seeing kids supported by other coaches sends a very strong message. You go*

to Lake Placid, you know Larry's going to be there with a positive thing to [say to] your kid, and you wouldn't have any doubt about it. But that being seen by others sends a very strong message, that these kids are gonna be okay. And you don't see that in alpine. You won't find a kid from Pats Peak being coached by anyone from Franconia or anywhere else.[177]

This idea of everyone supporting and helping one another out is why many stay involved. As Picton noted, "It was a good community, and everyone involved was always encouraging each person's effort every time. Everyone's effort was always considered worthy, and people expressed that. So it was a very constructive, worthwhile experience, whether you excelled in the sport or not."

5

CONCLUSION

Ski jumping in the Northeast has faced numerous challenges in the way of its survival, but it continues to be a viable sport. In the 1970s and '80s, the pool of jumpers, coaches, officials and volunteers began to narrow. The Scandinavian influence that once powered ski jumping in the Northeast was diminishing with each passing generation. In addition, Bogataj's terrible crash in ABC's famous "Agony of Defeat" video caused many Americans to see ski jumping as a dangerous sport, and when the NCAA dropped ski jumping from the list of college sports, it had a big, negative effect on ski jumping across the country. However, the Olympics serve as a constant inspiration to ski jumpers, and the success of influencing the IOC to incorporate women's ski jumping in the Olympics has gone a long way to broaden its appeal and beat inequality in the sport. Furthermore, the importance of tradition in the ski jumping community and the dedication of volunteers each winter keeps ski jumping at the local and regional levels afloat.

There is something intangible about ski jumping that captivates people. Mark Picton described the thirty- and sixty-five-meter jumps in Salisbury:

> *It takes place in a clearing in the woods on rickety-looking thrown-together trestles made out of old telephone poles and weathered boards, and the same thing for the sixty—it was a homemade tower just sticking up into the sky, and when you look at it when there isn't snow on it, it looks sort of derelict, but then when they have it all snowed and groomed and a track*

cut, it's this gleaming parabolic curve that somehow looks perfect, and it's the contradiction between the rough means and the surreally beautiful finish to it which is really kind of inspiring.[178]

This ability to captivate draws entire communities of volunteers, spectators and fans back to the sport year after year. Carey Fiertz of SWSA, who helps at the top of the tower during Jumpfest weekend, wrote in 2018,

It is humbling to contemplate the legion of volunteers and community supporters who have made this possible over the past 91 years. As I look from the tower over the town of Salisbury and across the valley to the distant hills, occasionally catching a whiff of the bonfires and hearing the ringing of cowbells, I feel like I am standing on the shoulders of giants. Some of the work we volunteers do is physically demanding, but nothing compared to the labor provided by our predecessors. We have snow guns and Sno-Cats and iPhones; they mostly had pails and shovels. The new steel tower is probably one of the most solid structures in town—the previous one, well, I still shudder thinking about that rickety old thing swaying with the most gentle breeze and seemingly held together with little more than rusty nails and baling wire.[179]

The old ski jump in Berlin, New Hampshire, Nansen, is also experiencing a renewal of interest in its proposed comeback after decades of disuse. Bolstered by town support as well as enthusiasm from the whole eastern jumping community, the Nansen jump was patched up just enough to make it safe for Sarah Hendrickson, Olympian and New Hampshire native, to jump it in 2017. The *Concord Monitor* read: "A towering piece of New Hampshire's history will be temporarily restored to active duty this month, when the 80-year-old Nansen Ski Jump launches one last skier. A team of Bow-based contractors spent six weeks this winter putting a new deck on the rotted, 171-foot-tall steel-framed structure, which was once the epicenter of American ski jumping."[180] New Hampshire's Cooper Dodds also snuck in an off-the-record jump on Nansen following Sarah's jump, becoming the second to jump the hill in decades. The Town of Berlin hopes to raise enough money to replace the tower and bring Nansen back to its prominent place on the eastern ski jumping circuit.

Heistad, who is now in his eighties, volunteers as a coach at the ski jumps in Lebanon. When asked why he stays involved, he said, "I think it's getting people to know that they can do things, beyond what they've done....We do

Takeoff of the Nansen Ski Jump, likely taken during the 1939 FIS World Championship and Olympic Tryouts. *Warren Chivers Archive.*

things because we can share in some other way the joy that somebody has in doing something for the first time, or the hundredth."[181] Heistad noted the importance of cultivating and keeping volunteers involved as vital to clubs' survival. Once, he met a couple who said they were interested in helping out in Lebanon. He recalled,

I said, "You want to volunteer? Go on and tell them in the kitchen that you want to volunteer." I saw them at a meet later, and they said "a woman in there told us that they're all set and they didn't need any help." And you know? I don't know as they ever came back again. They certainly didn't come back and volunteer. But that isn't the way you're gonna build the club. It isn't the way you're gonna build volunteers; it isn't the way people are gonna say, "Yeah, I know a really neat place, you oughta go there!" It's our own attitude we present to others, and if we don't give them that "Wow, thank you for being here" feeling, they don't feel it. It doesn't just come. You have to tell them. You have to let them know that they are important. And if you feel important some place, pretty soon you'll go back.[182]

In addition to the volunteer support that is crucial to ski jumping in the Northeast, the sense of camaraderie keeps the ski jumping community in place; everyone supporting one another creates an atmosphere that keeps people around. Larry Stone has coached for decades and will always encourage any jumper who walks his way. When asked what it is about ski jumping that makes him stay with it, he said, "Whether it's winning an event or the actual feeling of flying, it's such a physical and psychological rush.… If you've had some success and you've had that feeling of flying, it lasts the rest of your life. I get it through my kids. I take every jump my kids take, and you do too, I'm sure."[183] Caroline Gilbert of SWSA wrote:

The community of ski jumping is a model of commitment and volunteerism.…Everyone pitches in to shovel, judge, pick up skis and support the jumpers. Giving back is part of the culture. The small, close-knit community supports all its members, no matter the competency or age.… If your equipment needs adjustment, breaks or is faulty, team members and even competitors go out of their way to help find a new set of skis for you to be able to participate. Coaches share their knowledge with every jumper. It does not matter what club or team you are on, each jumper will have a coach at every hill who cares about everyone having fun and improving. Sometimes your child's coach is an Olympian.[184]

Perhaps the tight-knit atmosphere that promotes the volunteers, community support and camaraderie is due to the fact that the eastern ski jumping community is so small. Where there were once dozens of ski jumps marking the landscape throughout the Northeast, there are now just a few. Numerous ski jumping clubs that once existed in the metropolitan area are gone. Ski jumps at one time dotted every other town in Connecticut and Massachusetts, and now, Salisbury is the single remaining active jump in southern New England. Massachusetts has no ski jumps at all. In Lebanon, New Hampshire, the eight neighborhood jumps Heistad remembers have shrunk to just two.

These surviving jumps, however, carry a great responsibility to continue the tradition of ski jumping in the Northeast. Each club must do what it can to keep its volunteers motivated and its jumpers having fun, as Heistad notes: "I think the fun factor is what we really need to concentrate on. We don't have to worry about the official factor nearly as much as the fun factor. And we can strive for perfection in a wide variety of ways, but it's seldom that we ever really need it or have to have it. We can do a lot of things with something less than perfect."[185]

PART II

JUMPS OF THE NORTHEAST

ACTIVE JUMPS

NEW HAMPSHIRE

Andover | Andover Outing Club, Proctor Academy (Blackwater Ski Area)

Ski jumping came to Andover in the 1950s when Proctor Academy, a private boarding school located in the center of town, built ski jumps and started a jumping team.[186] Proctor maintained a twenty- and a thirty-meter jump for high school students for several decades before the Andover Outing Club (AOC) was founded, which has operated in conjunction with Proctor Academy's ski jumping team ever since.[187] Today, AOC and Proctor Academy share the use of their ten-meter, eighteen-meter, thirty-meter and thirty-eight-meter ski jumps.

The AOC's inception can be credited with the rejuvenation of ski jumping in Andover. In 1976, Tim Norris, an English teacher at Proctor at the time, started the AOC when his seven-year-old son expressed interest in learning to jump. Norris was a former jumper himself, having competed at the Dublin School in southern New Hampshire in slalom, giant slalom, cross-country and ski jumping. He went on to coach and mentor ski jumping and Nordic combined athletes for both Proctor Academy and Andover Outing Club for over forty years, retiring in 2018.[188] He maintained the philosophy that "the worst athlete needs to feel as important as the best—if not more—because otherwise, why are we doing this?"[189]

Andover Outing Club started out small, with just a few ski jumpers and cross-country skiers. They used the facilities at Blackwater Ski Area, which is owned by Proctor Academy. The area had cross-country and alpine trails and, at the time, just two jumps: a ten-meter and an eighteen-meter. Norris worked hard to develop the program, soon attracting and recruiting jumpers from a larger area including Concord, New London and Franklin. At first, the club ran on small donations made by neighbors and skiers' families, but once the program expanded, AOC began charging membership fees each season, which kept the club afloat. In the late 1990s, Marianne Fairall, mother of Olympic ski jumper Nick Fairall, began to take over the AOC administration on a volunteer basis, organizing almost every aspect of club activities alongside Norris, until she passed away in 2008.[190]

Several renovations and upgrades were made to the AOC jumps over the years, and in 1997, Norris oversaw the construction of a thirty-eight-meter jump at the facility. For the new hill, AOC was given telephone poles from TDS Telecom for the jump tower, and a contractor donated the lumber.

The Andover Outing Club and Proctor Academy jumps, 2021. *By Cooper Dodds.*

With help from AOC families and coaches, the jump was completed in just a few months, in time for a Christmas camp on the new hill. In 1998, a thirty-meter jump was built next to the thirty-eight, sharing a landing hill and the trestle with the thirty-eight.[191]

Norris coached and helped develop some of the country's top ski jumpers, including five Olympians: ski jumpers Carl Van Loan, Nick Fairall and Jed Hinkley and cross-country skiers Kris and Justin Freeman. As Hinkley pointed out, "You wouldn't believe that it (AOC) could produce Olympic caliber skiers, but that is the magic of Tim."[192]

Almost all credit for the success of the AOC jumping program can be given to Norris. An article in *The Dubliner* highlighted Norris's induction into the Ski Jumping Hall of Fame: "In years where snow was scarce, everyone could count on Tim's Proctor Academy hills having snow. In years where athletes were scarce, event organizers could count on having Tim's skiers from AOC at their tournaments. And whatever Tim might have had—skiers, facilities, and knowledge—it was always shared generously and with a smile."[193]

In 2018, Norris retired from his coaching post, and his former AOC and Proctor Academy jumping athlete Chris Jones took over as coach. Jones rejuvenated the Proctor Academy jumping team, which had waned in the previous couple years,[194] and also coaches young jumpers at AOC. The club holds "learn to ski jump" camps at the beginning of each winter season and, in addition to hosting high school jumping competitions, holds an annual eastern meet for clubs all around the Northeast.

Hanover | Ford Sayre (Oak Hill, Roger Burt Memorial Ski Jumps)

An important training venue for ski jumpers in the Northeast is in Hanover, located in the state's Upper Valley region. The Ford K. Sayre Memorial Ski Council operates a ski jumping complex at Oak Hill called the Roger Burt Memorial Ski Jumps that includes a twenty-meter and a thirty-two-meter jump. The twenty-meter can also serve as a ten-meter jump for beginners when skiers start halfway down the inrun. The property is owned by Dartmouth College and located a few miles outside of the town of Hanover.

The site of these jumps, Oak Hill, was once a small ski area established in the late 1930s for Dartmouth College students to use and train on. The area had its own ski patrol and included several ski jumps, a J-Bar lift, various ski tows, skating and a ski school program.[195]

The Ford K. Sayre Memorial Ski Council was named after Ford Sayre, a 1933 Dartmouth graduate who did much to introduce and popularize skiing in New Hampshire's Upper Valley. In the early 1930s, along with another Dartmouth alum, Sayre refurbished an old lumber camp stable, turning it into the Dartmouth-at-Moosilauke cabin at Jobilunk Ravine. Sayre and his wife, Peggy, kept the "Ravine Camp" running, mostly for use by Dartmouth students and alumni. Sayre also started a children's ski program at the Ravine Camp and became the first chairman of the Committee to Certify Professional Ski Instructors. The committee was a significant early step in the development of skiing in the country. In 1936, Sayre and his family moved to Hanover, where they ran a ski school and taught skiing at the Spy Glass Hill Farm the next year. In later years, Sayre ran ski schools out of the Hanover Inn, which he and his wife operated.[196]

In the late 1930s, the Sayres took over the Hanover Children's Carnival, a winter carnival started in 1917 in conjunction with the Hanover Inn and the Dartmouth Outing Club. This popular event featured ski jumping, speed and figure skating on Occom Pond and cross-country and downhill ski racing.[197]

In 1942, Ford Sayre enlisted in the U.S. Army Air Corps and went to war. Two years later, recently promoted from first lieutenant to captain, he died in a plane crash at the age of thirty-four. Back home, Peggy Sayre started the Ford Sayre Memorial Fund in honor of her late husband, devoted to providing free ski and jumping lessons for children who could not afford them. In 1945, this became the Ford Sayre Memorial Ski School and then the Ford Sayre Memorial Ski Council in 1950. The year after the ski school was formed, over one thousand children signed up for ski and ski jumping lessons. Equipment could be rented or borrowed, and the council collected equipment donations in a nearby barn.[198]

The current jumps at Oak Hill were named after Roger Burt, an Olympic judge at the 1969 Olympics who taught ski jumping to many youngsters in the Upper Valley.[199] By the 1980s, Dartmouth had closed the Oak Hill Ski Area down because the college had begun using a larger area for its students to train on.[200] In 1981, the Ford K. Sayre Memorial Ski Council took over operations of Oak Hill. With donations from local residents, Dartmouth College and the Town of Hanover, the council was able to replace the old J-Bar with a T-Bar, purchase used grooming equipment and make improvements to the ski jumps. With these improvements came a renewed interest in the skiing programs offered by the council and especially in the skimeister meets, which included events in four different skiing disciplines, including ski jumping.[201] The council continued to provide skiing and ski

Roger Burt Memorial Ski Jumps, 2021. *By Cooper Dodds.*

jumping lessons and equipment to children who could not afford to pay, while increasing membership fees to stay afloat.[202]

Today, the council provides free beginner ski jumping lessons several nights a week in the winter. Coached by Joe Holland, Mike Holland and Heidi Nichols, new jumpers use their downhill equipment and start just below the takeoff of the smallest jump. Those who wish to join the club have access to a large supply of ski jumping equipment provided by the club. Tom Dodds coaches Hanover High School jumpers on the larger thirty-two-meter jump.[203] Each winter, the council hosts a meet on the Roger Burt jumps, inviting clubs from around the Northeast to join in the competition. There is often a fire burning to keep jumpers and families warm, and cookies and hot chocolate are for sale at the warming hut by the takeoff of the thirty-two-meter jump.

Gilford | Gunstock Nordic Association

The four ski jumps making up the Gunstock jumping complex in Gilford were important training and competition hills for ski jumpers in the Northeast for many decades. Gunstock had ten-, twenty-, forty- and seventy-meter hills and maintained an active and successful junior and senior ski

Gunstock's sixty-meter jump, 1950s. *Courtesy of Becky Pingree.*

jumping program run under the Gunstock Nordic Association, previously the Gunstock Nordic Federation and the Gilford Outing Club.[204]

Gunstock's largest hill was built by the Works Progress Administration under Franklin Roosevelt's New Deal in 1937, originally built as a 60-meter jump with the capacity to hold five thousand spectators in the grandstand and four thousand cars in the parking area. In his history of the Gunstock jumps, Gary Allen writes, "In 1937–1938, they had 100 men building the 60 meter ski jump at the area [originally called the Belknap Recreation Area]. At that time in the development of ski jumps, it was a very modern hill." Right away, the new jump hosted big national and regional jumping competitions, and by 1940, Gunstock was holding meets with international competitors. In 1941, Torger Tokle jumped 76.5 meters, setting a hill record that held for the next thirty-five years. These large-scale competitions were held by the Winnipesaukee Ski Club, which was founded in 1918 and had operated several small jumps in the Gilford area since then. The 60-meter jump was accompanied by two junior jumps, a 10- and a 20-meter.[205]

In 1947, Gary Allen, Gus Pitou and Marty Hall Sr. founded the Gilford Outing Club. With the help of Allen, who purchased jumping skis and equipment from Norway in 1951, a Nordic rental program was established for those learning to jump. For five dollars, a jumper could rent skis and boots for the season.[206]

Though Gunstock's sixty-meter jump was used consistently through most of the 1950s, in 1958 the big hill went dormant and wasn't used again until 1970. Increased interest in alpine skiing in the 1950s and 1960s had hurt the Nordic program, but luckily two dedicated men, Gary Allen and Bill Trudgeon, continued to coach young jumpers on the ten- and twenty-meter hills during this time.[207]

From 1946 to 1975, Allen was the Nordic coach for Gunstock, running numerous competitions at the hills over the years. In 1969, the Gunstock Nordic Federation was established for young jumpers, and two years later the Gunstock Nordic Association (GNA) was founded for older jumpers and competitors. In 1972, the two groups joined into one organization. That year, GNA rebuilt all four hills under the management of Gary Allen, Pete Kling and Phil Allen, installing lights on the smaller hills and upgrading to modern ski jump profiles, which included grading all the hills and rebuilding the steel trestle for the big hill. The sixty-meter was upgraded to a seventy-meter and was certified to International Federation of Skiing (FIS) standards, with added starts, an extended inrun and a new four-story judges stand.[208]

The new renovations had a dramatic effect on GNA's activity: in 1975, the club had grown to include forty-five junior jumpers, and from 1974 to the early 1990s, GNA held large-scale national and international competitions on the big hill almost every year. Among these was the 1980 FIS International, hosting many of the best jumpers in the world ahead of the Lake Placid Olympics that year. In 1976, Allen introduced snowmaking on the jumping hills and developed a better way to pack and groom the landing hill and outrun of the jumps, with a two-ton roller on a winch and cable system. Allen recalled his first snowmaking attempt: "I got the snow guns from the alpine slopes at Gunstock, the fire hose from the fire department, and I rented a compressor from Milo Pike. I set it all up, and we put a suction pump into the reservoir up above Gunstock's 70 meter hill. It was just a Rube Goldberg setup which we rigged."[209]

The official hill record for the seventy-meter jump was made by Taylor Hoffman in 1994 with a jump of eighty-nine meters, and GNA sent several of its jumpers on to compete at the highest levels of the sport, including Teyck Weed to the Nordic Combined Olympic Team of 1972 and Glenn Joyce to the U.S. National Nordic Combined Team from 1977 to 1980.[210]

In recent years, jumping at Gunstock has been scaled back, due to a lack of funding and help. Allen commented on these issues:

> *One thing I find which has always bothered me, is that our (ski) area tends to invest only in alpine. It's like pulling hens' teeth to get them to spend*

anything on nordic....One nice thing about the old days is that most of us were volunteers. In those days, you could get any number of fathers out to teach the kids, run the ski tow, and pack the slopes....In recent times, volunteering has not been popular.[211]

These days, beginners can try jumping on a small jump, but the bigger hills are no longer used.

Newport | Roland Tremblay Ski Jumping Complex

The town of Newport, located in western New Hampshire near Mount Sunapee Resort, is home to the Roland Tremblay Ski Jumping Complex, which holds three jumps: a ten-meter, a twenty-five-meter and a thirty-meter, accessible to the school districts of Newport, Kearsarge and Sunapee, all with high school ski jumping teams. Competitions on the hills are also featured in an annual Newport Winter Carnival, held in February.[212]

Above and opposite: Newport's thirty-meter jump, 2021. *By Cooper Dodds.*

Ski jumping in Newport dates back to 1916, when the local YMCA and the Newport Outing Club hosted the first Winter Carnival. The activities began early in the afternoon with skiers, ice skaters and snowshoers parading to local resident Bella Cutting's meadow, just north of Newport Middle School. Among the events was a toboggan slide a third of a mile long. The following year, the carnival included a seven-mile sleigh ride to Blue Mountain Forest Park where carnival goers joined in a deer drive on snowshoes. The festivities continued into the evening with a dinner, a concert and ball at the opera house and, finally, a bonfire.[213]

In 1967, a twenty-meter jump was built by Newport High School, a project spearheaded by Coach Ted Niboli for his Newport High School ski team. This was the first jump built at the high school location. Money for the project was donated by Newport residents, while Coach Niboli and team members contributed to the construction of the jump. A second thirty-meter jump was built at the high school in 1972, spearheaded by Roland Tremblay, John C. McCrillis, Robert Rollins, Frank MacConnell and James Lantz.[214] In 1976, a new tower for the thirty-meter ski jump was moved to Newport from the Lake Placid ski jumping complex.[215]

The hill is named for Roland Tremblay, who coached and maintained the Newport High School ski jumping program for more than thirty years and was an eastern and national ski jumping judge and official.[216] An important training venue, the Newport jumps are integral to the survival of high school ski jumping in New Hampshire.

Conway | Mount Washington Valley Ski Jumping

Carved out of the banks of the Kancamagus Highway are two ski jumps run by nearby Kennett High School. The Kennett High Ski Jumping Team trains on the twenty- and thirty-eight-meter hills here during the short days of winter, after school and usually under the lights. *New Hampshire Magazine* describes the scene on one competition evening in 2013:

> *The Kancamagus Highway, a hilly, winding, fun road between Conway and Lincoln in the North Country, is justly famous for its sweeping vistas of glorious fall color. On a chilly late-February night, however, the Kanc is in a darker mood as you leave Conway and head west, as you follow your headlights through a canyon of tall, silent stands of solitary pine and fir and spruce, all motionless and black and slightly sinister. Then parked cars line both sides of the road, people scurry about, and suddenly an eerie, brilliant, blinding light floods a huge cave carved out of the black forest. Is this an alien landing? No, it's a ski jump! Right there in nowhere, and it's the site of the New Hampshire State High School Ski Jumping Championships—the "States," to the youthful competitors. The Big One.[217]*

Originally built in 1960, the jump was upgraded in 1990, and in 2009, the Conway School District acquired the jumping venue from the Kennett Company.

Ski jumping has a long history in the Conway area. In January 1922, North Conway held the first White Mountains Winter Sports Carnival,

Mount Washington Valley Ski Jumps in Conway, 2021. *By Cooper Dodds.*

featuring ice hockey, skijoring and snowshoeing events, dogsled races and horse races down Main Street. A ski jump was built especially for the events, erected at the bottom of Cathedral Ledge on West Side Road. Around five hundred spectators watched the jumping event during the carnival that year. Just north of Conway in the town of Intervale, there was once a forty-meter jump by a ski hill. The ski area was started by Fred Pabst in the mid-1930s, but by the mid-1960s the ski jump was taken down.[218]

Today, high school competitions at the Kennett jump draw big crowds of families and friends, proud to ring cowbells in support of their local jumping teams. Hot chocolate and snacks are sold at meets by local Boy Scouts and the Kennett Key Club, and raffles are organized to support the team. Grace Ward, a ski jumper for Kennett High School, writes: "If you ever attend a Kennett meet you will see a massive bonfire, young kids watching the jumpers and playing on the snow banks as well as parents, grandparents and alumni. Everyone loves to watch their friends and family hurl themselves off the jump."[219]

Plymouth | Plymouth High (Bobcat Hill)

The Plymouth Regional High School has two ski jumps for the school's jumping team: an eighteen-meter and a twenty-eight-meter, both built in 2015, replacing a smaller hill that had been the school's ski jump since 1979.

The high school's first jump, a twenty-four-meter hill, was constructed by Norm Leblanc, a construction trades teacher and coach at the school, with help from a group of students including Bill Hendrickson, father of elite ski jumper Sarah Hendrickson, and Gene Ross, who would later become the ski jumping coach for Plymouth High School. In September 2015, the twenty-four-meter jump was inspected for structural stability and found to be unsafe, so the school board voted to tear it down, citing a lack of funds to rebuild or repair the jump. Without a jump on campus, parents and former coach Leblanc knew the high school team would suffer; they would have to travel an hour to Proctor Academy's ski jump in Andover, New Hampshire, to train. Furthermore, without the visibility of having a jump right on campus, they worried that local interest in ski jumping would fade.[220]

Fearing that Plymouth's jumping team would be lost, Leblanc and Skip Johnstone, parent of a Plymouth High ski jumper, spearheaded a movement

The Gene Ross Memorial Ski Jump, 2016. *Courtesy of Sean Hurley.*

to raise money to have the jump rebuilt.[221] Quickly, the fundraising effort exceeded their goal of $50,000. Johnstone started a Facebook group called "Save Our Ski Jump" that received donations from all over the world. Plymouth High School students solicited donations from around the community, a local contractor offered to demolish the old jump for free and an engineering firm designed the new jump. Sarah Hendrickson spoke at a fundraiser in November and helped raise another $12,000.[222] In just a couple months, the group raised more than $78,000. The new jump was completed by Thanksgiving of the same year, aided by volunteer labor from within the community. The school installed new lighting as well as security fencing around the jump. The new jump reenergized interest in the student body for ski jumping, and the team nearly doubled in size that year.[223]

The jump was named the Gene Ross Memorial Ski Jump in honor of Plymouth High School's ski jumping coach from 1992 to 2003. Ross, who passed away in 2003, was captain of the Plymouth High School Ski Jumping Team from 1979 to 1981 and took part in the construction of the jump in 1979.[224]

The rebuilding of the Plymouth jump is an inspiring example of the large role local communities can have in the future of ski jumping. In this case, the huge community support for the project also helped to keep high school ski jumping viable in New Hampshire, the only remaining state to sanction the sport at this level.

Lebanon | Lebanon Outing Club (Storrs Hill)

Lebanon Outing Club (LOC) is home to Heistad Hill, a fifty-meter ski jump, whose steel frame rises impressively high over the landscape. One look at the jump from the parking lot is enough to send the fainthearted packing. Along with the fifty-meter hill is a twenty-five-meter jump and an eight-meter jump for beginner and intermediate ski jumpers. Located near the heart of Lebanon, New Hampshire, the ski jumps are part of Storrs Hill, a small, volunteer-run ski hill with a Poma lift to the top. At the base of the hill is a lodge with picnic tables and a small kitchen where skiers can buy snacks, candy and drinks. Out in front of the lodge, ski racks fill up on a Friday night with new race skis, old straight skis, tele skis and jumping skis, which tower over the others by several feet. At the top of Storrs Hill, a giant star is lit up at night, and from the top of the hill a skier can view the entire city of Lebanon.

ANNUAL REPORT
Town of
LEBANON, NEW HAMPSHIRE
1940

Lebanon's thirty-five-meter jump, 1940. *Courtesy of Betty Ann Heistad.*

In 1923, a twenty-six-year-old teacher named Erling Heistad moved to the town, bringing his home country's sport with him. Originally from Tonsberg, Norway,[225] Heistad came to Lebanon to take a teaching position. Believing that there should be a ski jump in every neighborhood, Heistad started building jumps. When he was done, he'd designed and built eight ski jumps across the town. The hill Heistad initially built at Storrs Hill was a thirty-five-meter jump, but in 1954 he replaced it with the current steel structured fifty-meter hill. Heistad's son Erling recalled his father's reaction when the new jump was dedicated to him: "There's a plaque on the front of the jump that says 'dedicated to…' and all that stuff…but it came out in the paper as the ski jump 'dedicated in memorial to.'…So dad's reading the paper the next morning and he says, 'That's pretty funny, not everybody can sit and read the paper about their own memorial!'"[226]

Except for Storrs Hill, the neighborhood jumps are all gone, but there are still remnants of takeoffs and landing hills here and there, if you know where to look. Erling recalled that his father "built a jump just up from where the Heistad Hill is, up the stream. There was a place with a dam, and everybody called it 'The Scrape,' because if you dove in the water and you didn't dive shallow enough, you'd scrape your belly."[227] In the 1920s, Heistad (Sr.) started out by making skis in the school shop for his students to use. Then he approached Northlands, a local toboggan maker, to see if it would make jumping skis for him. Though Northlands was at first skeptical, the company ended up making jumping skis for the next twenty-five or thirty years for jumpers in Lebanon.[228]

Heistad coached ski jumping along with slalom, downhill and cross-country skiing from 1923 to 1947 and established the Lebanon Outing Club along the way. He coached Lebanon High School teams, "develop[ing] some of the country's foremost skiers and coaches and send[ing] them to colleges as top athletes in all four skiing sports."[229] Heistad had the students and skiers he coached help him construct and maintain ski trails and jumps

Snowmaking on Lebanon Outing Club's Heistad Hill, 2016. *By Ariel Kobayashi.*

as part of their training regimen and to instill in his students a feeling of ownership and responsibility for their home jump.[230] In addition to his duties as a coach, Heistad was an eastern ski jumping judge, a national judge and an official at the 1960 Winter Olympics in Squaw Valley, California.[231]

Cameron Summerton skiing through the Hoop of Fire during Lebanon Outing Club's Mud Meet, 2017. *By Gary Summerton.*

Heistad also designed ski jumps, free of charge, for schools and universities, including Norwich University, University of Vermont, Holderness Academy and New Hampton School.[232]

In the fall of 1947, Heistad recruited Al Merril to take over some of his coaching duties at Lebanon Outing Club. Heistad's son Erling also coached jumping, along with Bernie and Roger Dion, Jon Farnham, Nick Burke and Ed Tourville. Erling, now in his eighties, is still a volunteer coach for the twenty-five-meter jump.

For years, Storrs Hill was run and operated by the City of Lebanon, but in the 1980s the expenses to insure and continue operating the ski hill became too much for the city to handle. Responsibility for the site fell into the hands of Lebanon Outing Club volunteers who wanted to keep their beloved neighborhood ski hill running. Volunteers now perform the grooming, snowmaking and coaching, and run the ticket sales, the Poma lift and the ski patrol.[233]

The club hosts a January Junior Championships qualifying ski jumping event on the fifty-meter hill, and the famous Mud Meet in March, which features jumping on all three hills and a skimeister meet, which is a competition for best all-round skier in downhill, cross-country, and ski jumping. The Mud Meet closes each year with the highly anticipated "Hoop of Fire." A flaming hoop is secured at the takeoff of the twenty-five-meter jump, and after the official competition, young jumpers ski through it just before launching off the takeoff.

In 2017, Lebanon Outing Club was the first in the Northeast to install steel tracks on the inruns of its twenty-five- and fifty-meter jumps. The steel tracks can replace a snow inrun, making hill maintenance in the winter easier, and this was a big step toward creating a venue for ski jumpers to train year-round in New England. The next step is installing plastic grass on the landing hills of the jump, which they hope to accomplish in the coming years.

Berlin | (Nansen Ski Jump)

The Nansen Ski Jump rises like a beacon of the past near the town line between Berlin and Milan, its 172-foot steel tower reaching high above Route 16 and the Androscoggin River.[234]
—New Hampshire Union Leader

On the edge of New Hampshire's White Mountains, the city of Berlin is the northernmost in the state, located in the Great North Woods Region. In the mid-1800s, newly arrived Norwegian immigrants began to settle here, finding work at the local sawmill owned by the Berlin Mills Company.

Berlin's was the first ski club in the Northeast. While there is some argument as to whether its founding date was 1872 or 1882, the club was founded in Berlin by a group of Norwegians, including ski maker Olaf Oleson.[235] They initially named their new organization the Berlin Mills Skiklubben after the town's main industry but changed the name to the Berlin Mills Ski Club and then again in 1905 to the Fridtjof Nansen Ski Club, named after the famous explorer who was the first to cross Greenland on skis in 1888.[236]

The club's first competition was a cross-country race, held in 1882. The first jump in Berlin was built in 1890 close to the Androscoggin River, which runs through town, and supported jumps of up to 55 feet in length. Over the next few years, a series of larger ski jumps and cross-country trails were built across town, and in 1922, the club held its first winter carnival, building a 125-foot jump for the event. This jump was then moved and enlarged to a 150-foot jump. Initially, the Nansen Ski Club accepted only fellow Norwegians into the club, but by 1912 it began allowing non-Norwegians to become members.[237] Skiing and ski jumping quickly became central to life in Berlin. The club sponsored large-scale national tournaments and winter carnivals and in 1926 held a cross-country race 100 miles long.[238]

An early ski jumping star of the Nansen Ski Club was Ingvald "Bing" Anderson, setting hill records in Lake Placid and Brattleboro in the early 1920s. He became famous across the Northeast. The *Journal of the New England Ski Museum* recalls that he "was a ski jumping hero to children in Berlin—'the finest jumper of his time.'" Sadly, his name is also associated with a darker story, as the *Journal* again relates: "Anderson's frequent ski jumping triumphs were punctuated by equally recurrent periods of inactivity as an inmate of the Coos County, New Hampshire jail, and in the end he was convicted of murder and executed in Nova Scotia in 1930."[239] Friends of Anderson had come to his aid, insisting on his mental instability and pleading for a more gentle sentence, to no avail.[240]

Another man well known in town was Alf Halvorson. An integral part of the development of the ski jump in Berlin, he became president of the Nansen Ski Club in 1917. He created the Junior Nansen Ski Club in the early 1920s to inspire children in Berlin to take up ski jumping and skiing.[241]

Later, in the mid-1930s, Halvorson served as director of the local chapter of the National Youth Administration (NYA) during the Depression and initiated the plan to construct a huge 80-meter ski jump, employing young men through the NYA to build the jump. The completed steel-framed jump cost $100,000 in construction and soared 171.5 feet high. The inrun was 310 feet long, and by the time a skier took flight they were often going 55 miles per hour. The inaugural event on the new jump was the 1938 Olympic Trials, which attracted a crowd of 25,000 onlookers and was broadcasted on 87 different radio stations.[242] The momentous event was attended by Governor Francis P. Murphy and several NYA officials who had traveled from Washington, D.C., for the event.

Although there were no official jumping events for women at the time, female jumper Johanne Kolstad from Norway entered and jumped Big Nansen during the inaugural event, flying seventy-two meters and setting the women's world record in ski jumping, a record that was not surpassed for more than thirty years.[243] Another woman to jump Nansen early on was Pearl Oleson, daughter of Olaf Oleson, one of the first Scandinavians to settle in Berlin in the 1800s. She and her brothers Clarence "Spike" and Alton Oleson were known to jump Nansen side by side, holding hands. Although there were no sanctioned competitions open to women, Pearl competed in Berlin's annual Winter Carnival events for the title of "Carnival Queen."[244]

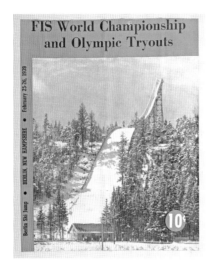

Poster for the 1939 FIS World Championship and Olympic Tryouts. *Warren Chivers Archive.*

This jump came to be known as "Big Nansen" and, at the time of its construction, was the tallest ski jump tower in the world. Big Nansen and the Nansen Ski Club hosted several major competitions, including the Olympic Trials, many Winter Carnival events and the U.S. National Ski Jumping Championships of 1940, 1957, 1965 and 1972. The *New Hampshire Union Leader* noted, "For decades, from the 1930s into the 1980s, spectators flocked to competitions here, gathering around the landing hill or watching the action from their parked cars below, where they'd listen to the commentary on the radio and honk car horns after a particularly good jump."[245]

In 1985, just over a decade after the last National Championships were held on the Big Nansen, the jump went dormant, not to be used again for thirty-two years.[246] The ski jumping scene in the United States had changed quickly in the 1980s after the NCAA dropped ski jumping as a sanctioned college sport, and with less support and fewer people around, the labor-intensive process of preparing a big jumping hill like Nansen became harder to pull off. On top of that, in 1977 a ski jumper from New England College took a fall during a practice jump on Nansen, leaving him paralyzed. He later sued the U.S. Ski Association and the Nansen Ski Club, along with some of its officers, which proved to be the finishing stroke for the Big Nansen's decades-long run.[247]

The jump was abandoned for several decades; the landing hill, outrun and clearing around the tower became so overgrown that eventually it was difficult to see even the tall tower through the trees. The *Journal of the New England Ski Museum* recounted, "The area around the landing hill, along Route 16, had become a dumping ground for everything from household trash to mattresses and rusty car parts.…The wooden decking on the jump was rotted away. But the memory of Nansen, and its legendary status, remained."[248]

In 2015, the state initiated efforts to restore the site, clearing the land and marking the jump as a New Hampshire Historic Site.[249] A group called the Friends of Nansen Ski Jump formed with the purpose of overseeing the jump and determining its future. When the energy drink company Red

The Nansen Ski Jump tower, likely decorated for the 1939 FIS World Championship and Olympic Tryouts. *Warren Chivers Archive.*

Nansen Ski Jump, 2017. *By Cooper Dodds.*

Bull caught a whiff of the small-scale efforts to clean up the historic site, it expressed interest in helping to finance a partial restoration of the jump so that ski jumper Sarah Hendrickson could take a jump off of Nansen for a documentary. With Red Bull's help, new decking was installed on the inrun, the landing hill was rebuilt, and after major struggles with the weather, the jump was ready and Hendrickson took her historic jump off of the Big Nansen, becoming the first person to jump the legendary hill in more than three decades.[250] The energy created by this partial restoration of the jump and the video of Sarah flying off the Big Nansen motivated an effort to fully restore the jump and bring it back to full use in the coming years.[251]

NEW YORK

Lake Placid | New York Ski Education Foundation (NYSEF)

The town of Lake Placid in the Adirondack Mountains is home to the two largest ski jumps in the Northeast and has hosted the Winter Olympics twice. Sitting at two thousand feet above sea level, surrounded by the highest peaks in New York and often enjoying the most snowfall among jumping towns, Lake Placid is arguably the capital of ski jumping in the Northeast.

Now well known for its legacy of winter sports, Lake Placid first began attracting tourists as a summer resort in the late 1800s. Once an arduous overnight journey from major cities, the trip to the small town was made easy by the railroads. Quickly, the lakeside village became a popular summer resort destination; even in 1883, a *New York Times* article noted the increase in visitors from major cities each season to the Adirondack Park: "Tourists turn with relief from the thought of hot, dusty, crowded Chicago [and New York] to the cool shades of the Adirondack woods," and "it is possible to go aboard a splendid Wagner car at the Grand Central Station in the evening and land at Lake Placid next morning."[252]

By the early twentieth century, Lake Placid was gaining traction as a winter sports hub: a 1916 *New York Times* article described the new winter destination: "In less than twelve hours after leaving the slushy streets of New York, with their trampled, muddy snow, the Winter lover finds himself in the heart of the everlasting hills in the centre of the 'Switzerland of America,' where outdoor sport is the order of the day, and the hotels, clubs, and dwelling houses are modern and comfortable."[253] Lake Placid was one of the first American resorts to become a winter destination, too, when the

Newly installed summer jumping surface on Lake Placid's seventy-meter hill: "plastic grass" was used on the landing hill and porcelain tracks on the inrun, 1980s. *Warren Chivers Archive.*

Lake Placid Club decided to keep a small clubhouse open throughout the winter of 1905.[254] The club was founded in 1895 by Dr. Melville Dewey as a recreational and social club, and its initial members were mostly teachers, writers, professors and librarians who valued the natural surroundings the Adirondacks had to offer.

Once enthusiasm for winter activities among Lake Placid Club members and beyond began to grow, Dewey started importing skis from Europe. He built skating rinks and toboggan runs for the guests' use, and he also built the first ski jumps in Lake Placid at Intervale, just outside of town,[255] as well as several other small jumps around town.[256] The construction of the Intervale thirty-five-meter jump cost the club $1,700, and the first jumping competition held there was hosted by the Lake Placid Club on February 21, 1921, with three thousand spectators.[257] In 1920, the Lake Placid Sno Birds group was formed to help promote the growing popularity of winter sports in town. The Sno Birds were responsible for bringing in ski instructors in 1921, and that same year, the group began hosting College Week, a winter carnival with jumping competitions for students from colleges and universities in the United States and Canada, held between Christmas and New Year's each year.[258]

In 1923, the thirty-five-meter jump at Intervale was reconstructed as a fifty-meter jump,[259] and four years later it was again improved into a sixty-meter jump, to better host a growing number of major national jumping competitions.[260] The Official Report of the Third Winter Games noted the changes made to the jump in 1927: "The upper hill was lengthened and the tower rebuilt in steel, 12 feet wide and 66 feet high, with two starting platforms....The total investment in the present 60-meter hill is approximately $35,000."[261]

Lake Placid's prominence as a winter sports hub in the country and its already notable history of national ski jumping competitions at the Intervale jump was a significant factor in the International Olympic Committee's decision to award Lake Placid with the hosting of the 1932 Third Winter Olympic Games, a huge honor to the Adirondack community and to the United States.[262] On February 4, 1932, athletes from seventeen nations—Austria, Belgium, Canada, Czechoslovakia, Finland, France, Germany, Great Britain, Hungary, Italy, Japan, Norway, Poland, Roumania, Sweden, Switzerland and the United States—joined together for the Opening Ceremonies. As the Olympic Official Report recalled,

The flags of the nations flew everywhere. Great hotels and clubs, cottages, private homes, and business houses, were brave with bunting. Adirondack greens and pillars and arches of clear, green ice lined the main streets.... There was a tenseness in the air as of something impending. Even before daylight, trains, automobiles, buses, and airplanes began disgorging great crowds of passengers....[263] Parading with military precision, the stride

Lake Placid's seventy-meter jump with the Sno Bird emblem on takeoff, circa 1955. *Courtesy of Jay Rand.*

Lake Placid's thirty-meter jump, 1960s. *Warren Chivers Archive.*

of many of the athletes showing that in other years they had marched in the uniforms of their countries to strains more martial than those at the Olympic stadium....It was the most impressive sight of the Games. The brilliant sun; the multi-colored uniforms, ranging from the somber blue of the Norwegians and the Japanese to the white of the Americans; the hum of an airplane overhead; the sparkling, blue ice; and the cloudless sky above all combined to produce a picture of Winter and his sons and daughters that those privileged to see it will remember always.[264]

The most popular events of the 1932 Games were the ski jumps, and they brought out the largest crowds of the Olympics; ten thousand watched as Norway swept the field, with Birger Ruud winning gold; Hans Beck, the new hill record holder, taking silver; and Kåre Walberg with the bronze.

In 1950, the large hill was used again for the Nordic World Ski Championship, and starting in the mid-1950s, the annual Kennedy Games were held in Lake Placid,[265] a yearly event similar to the Olympics, suggested by John F. Kennedy to increase "international understanding."[266]

Lake Placid hosted the Winter Olympics again in 1980. Two brand-new ski jumps, a seventy-meter and a ninety-meter, designed by Karl Martitsch, were constructed specifically for the event. Construction began in May 1977, to be ready for a 1979 pre-Games test competition. The jumps were built

Lake Placid's seventy-meter jump, circa 1932. *Courtesy of Jay Rand.*

with concrete towers and steel inruns. Wood planking lined the inrun to hold snow. Over three hundred tons of steel was used on the inruns, and the larger of the two jumps included a glass encapsulated elevator for transporting jumpers and officials to the top of the tower. Due to a lack of natural snow, that year, manmade snow was used on the jumps. A model 3700 Thiokol diesel-powered snow cat that was specifically designed for use on ski jumps was employed to push, pack and grade the landing hills and outruns. A self-winding winch mounted on the back of the snow cat pulled the machine up the steep landing hills and lowered it down again and "literally took the place of 50 men," the Olympic Official Report noted.[267]

Lake Placid frequently held ski jumping World Cup events on both hills. In the early 1980s, the seventy-meter jump was covered in plastic surface for use in the summer, and a K48 and K18 were also built, complete with the summer plastic surface for year-round training. In 1986, the Junior World Ski Championships were held at the Lake Placid jumping complex, and in 1994 the large jumps were updated and reprofiled as K90 and K120. In 2011, the K18 was moved and rebuilt as a K20 between the K48 and K120, and in 2019, both the K90 and K120 were updated with refrigerated tracks on the inrun, making winter training on both hills much more feasible and consistent.[268]

CONNECTICUT

Salisbury | Salisbury Winter Sports Association (Satre Hill)

The ski jumps in Salisbury, Connecticut, are nestled into a wooded hillside just on the edge of town. A sixty-five-meter jump towers above the tops of the pines, and off to the side are two smaller jumps: a twenty-meter and a thirty-meter, used by younger jumpers. Practices on the smaller hills are held throughout the winter, and Salisbury hosts a yearly festival-like competition weekend in February called Jumpfest. On this weekend, jumpers from all over the Northeast compete on the K65 in a nighttime "Target Jump" under the lights on Friday, the "Salisbury Invitational" on Saturday and the "Eastern Championships" on Sunday. On Saturday morning, younger jumpers compete on the smaller hills. Based on Sunday's results on the big hill, some qualify for the Junior Championships, a national event held a few weeks later.

Ski jumping in Salisbury dates back to the 1920s. In 1925, Johan (John) Satre, who had recently emigrated from Trysil, Norway, settled in Salisbury, Connecticut. A rural area of rolling farmland and hills, Salisbury must have reminded Satre of Norway, and he soon decided to introduce his country's favorite sport to the people of Salisbury. In 1926, in front of a crowd of two hundred or more, Satre sailed off the roof of a barn on his skis to demonstrate ski jumping to the curious onlookers.[269]

Cameron Forbush on Salisbury Winter Sports Association's sixty-five-meter hill during Jumpfest, 2021. *By Savage Frieze.*

Soon, John's brothers Magnus, Olaf, Ottar and Sverre immigrated to America and joined John, who had already picked out a location for the first ski jump in town. The brothers had been competitive jumpers and cross-country skiers in Norway, and together with the help of Norwegian immigrants Birger Torrissen and Ole Hegge, they inspired excitement for ski jumping in Connecticut. By 1927, the three jumps had been built, and in 1932, the Olympic ski jumping trials were held in Salisbury in front of eight thousand onlookers. The hill was named Satre Hill, after John.[270]

This core group of Norwegians started the Salisbury Outing Club, which became the Salisbury Winter Sports Association in 1945. Members jumped nationally and won recognition across the country.[271] A 1931 *New York Times* article read: "Salisbury, Conn., Jan. 25—Perpetuating the fame of the Satre family among the ski stars of the world, Ottar Satre of the Salisbury Outing Club leaped 152 feet to win the Connecticut jumping championship in the closing event of the State's fifth annual championship ski meet here yesterday and today."[272] The Salisbury Outing Club also taught locals like Roy Sherwood, who, born in Salisbury in 1932, started at the age of seven and was jumping nationally at the highest level of the sport by the time he was eighteen.[273] In 1954, Sherwood became National Champion when he won the National Ski Jumping Championship in Ishpeming, Michigan.[274] Incredibly, though Sherwood contracted polio in 1954, he was able to work through the effects of the debilitating disease and went on to qualify for and compete in the 1956 Winter Olympics in Cortina, Italy. He continued to jump competitively for years afterward; in 1964, the *New York Times* reported his win at the famous ski jump in Bear Mountain, New York:

> *Jan. 5—Roy Sherwood, a 31-year-old highway maintenance worker from Salisbury, Conn., twice sailed through the air in fine fashion today to win the Norway Ski Club's annual ski jumping competition by a narrow margin. Performing on the Palisade Interstate Park's 50-meter hill before a record crowd of 36,124, Sherwood defeated Ralph Semb of Miller's Falls, Mass., by 1.5 points.[275]*

During World War II, when many of the young men involved in the club went overseas to fight, the ski jump in Salisbury went dormant and fell into disrepair. In December 1945, however, the Salisbury Winter Sports Association was established in an effort to rejuvenate Nordic sports in town. A new sixty-five-meter jump was built by 1949, and in 1950, Salisbury began holding the Eastern Ski Jumping Championships on the new jump.[276] A 1950 *New York*

Takeoff of Lake Placid's 120-meter jump, 2015. *By Cooper Dodds.*

Salisbury's sixty-five-meter hill, circa 1950. *By Ward Hutchinson, The Salisbury Association Photo Archive.*

Times article detailed the jump renovations: "The Salisbury hill has had a face-lifting so that leaps of 200 feet can be anticipated. The inrun has been built up, the take-off pushed back forty-five feet and the knoll has been filled in with earth, twenty-three feet above the old takeoff. The transition has been made steeper and the outrun lengthened and widened so that the hill today

The Salisbury Winter Sports Association ski jumps, 2021. *By Cooper Dodds.*

ranks with the best in the country."[277] Competitors on Satre Hill that year jumped in front of a huge crowd of ten thousand and included the Norwegian World Champion team, the Canadian team and the very best jumpers from the States.[278] The same *New York Times* article announced:

> *This pioneer ski community, seeking to regain some of its luster of the early Nineteen Thirties, will be in the limelight tomorrow when a brilliant collection of skiers takes off in the first international open jump on the Salisbury Outing Club's enlarged hill. Despite the lack of cooperation from the elements—the second year in a row—the local citizenry, farmers, industrialists and white collar men today were joined by some sixty talented jumpers in preparing the 800-foot-long incline with artificial snow. The countryside rocked with hilarity as the workers tossed bales of hay on the outrun and the flat, then covered it with the tons of pulverized ice blown out by an assortment of cutters. Even the farmers' trusted ensilage blower was utilized to spray portions of the chute otherwise nearly inaccessible due to the steepness of the pitch.[279]*

The tradition of ski jumping in Salisbury continued: young skiers were coached throughout the decades by veteran jumpers including the Satre brothers, Roy Sherwood, Larry Stone, Jon Swanson, Justin Hyack, Mark Breen and Ariel Picton. In 2009, the sixty-five-meter jump was replaced with a brand-new jump tower made of concrete and steel. The town of Salisbury came together to raise the $750,000 needed in a short amount of time so that Salisbury could host the Junior Nationals competitions in 2011. This outpouring of support proved that the ski jump had become an essential part of the community of Salisbury. In 2011, the *New York Times* wrote: "Sally Spillane, a resident of Salisbury, said: 'I've lived here for 28 years, and it takes a lot of things to make up a town. I think S.W.S.A. and ski jumping are a huge part of this kind of folk culture and tradition in our community.'"[280]

VERMONT

Brattleboro | Harris Hill Nordic (Harris Hill, Living Memorial Park)

The southern Vermont town of Brattleboro became a major center for skiing and ski jumping by the early twentieth century, largely due to a man named Fred Harris. Born in Brattleboro in 1887, Harris started skiing in 1904 and helped establish three important ski organizations: the Dartmouth Outing Club, the Brattleboro Outing Club and the US Eastern Amateur Ski Association (USEASA). The *Journal of the New England Ski Museum* credits Harris and these organizations as "provid[ing] the structure for the emerging sport of skiing that still endures today."[281]

In late 1909, while attending Dartmouth College, Harris founded the Dartmouth Outing Club.[282] After graduating, Harris established Brattleboro's first Winter Carnival in 1921[283] and played a large part in founding the Brattleboro Outing Club (BOC) in 1922, with the help of a town organization called the Brattleboro Community Service. Harris aimed to use his recent background to create a similar experience for ski enthusiasts in his hometown. In 1922, BOC built its first ski jump, a 60-meter hill. Construction of the jump cost $2,200, which Harris paid for himself.[284] It was built on property that belonged to a Vermont mental health hospital called the Brattleboro Retreat.[285] The BOC also established campsites and trails for summer use as well as the 40-mile Winged Ski Trail for skiing and hiking that, while short-lived, passed from Brattleboro to the Long Trail at Stratton Mountain.[286] In 1922, a new hill record of 158.5 feet was set by Ingvaled "Bing" Anderson, skiing out of Berlin, New

Brattleboro ski jump, 1930s. *Warren Chivers Archive.*

Hampshire. Anderson beat his own hill record three years later, soaring 190 feet on the Brattleboro jump.[287]

In an effort to introduce the sport of skiing to children, the Brattleboro Outing Club established a ski program in 1923 that included short cross-country tours, ski jump lessons on small jumps and telemark skiing classes.[288] The ski jump in Brattleboro attracted thousands of spectators and became a large force in the town's winter economy.[289] From 1924 to 1951, Brattleboro held five national ski jumping championships in which some of the premier jumpers in the world competed.[290] As a February 1924 *New York Times* pointed out during the Intercollegiate Ski Jumping Championship that year, "Class A and Class B ski jumping will bring together the largest number of high-class riders ever assembled in this country. More than fifty entrants are in the city tonight."[291] The championship held in 1924 was the first National Ski Jumping Championship to be held in the Northeast, an honor for BOC. The *Journal of the New England Ski Museum* noted that this "marked the beginning of an eastward tilt in the center of gravity of organized skiing."[292]

Over the next several decades, changes were gradually made to the hill. In 1929, a new tower was built for the ski jump, and in 1941 the hill was reprofiled. During World War II, there was no jumping at Harris Hill,

Harris Hill, 2020. *By Cooper Dodds.*

and in 1949 BOC replaced the previous wooden trestle inrun with a dirt mound.[293] During the fifth National Championships in Brattleboro, held in 1951, the ski jump was dedicated to Fred Harris. A member of the Brattleboro Outing Club recalled:

> *At its heyday in 1951, the National Championships were held on the hill for the fifth time, drawing a record 10,000 spectators to witness a contest comprised of a record field of 168 jumpers from around the globe. Art Tokle of Norway floated on the updraft to a new record of 239 feet. Fittingly, on that day, this historic hill, carved into an inconspicuous slope rising out of a cornfield, was re-dedicated in honor of its pioneering patron as Harris Hill.*[294]

A new tower was built in 1957 with a cost of $2,700, along with a new judges stand, and in 1974 Harris Hill was enlarged to a seventy-meter hill, adding two starts to the top of the inrun.[295] The very next year, tragedy struck when a member of the U.S. National Ski Jumping Team, Jeff Wright of Minneapolis, died from injuries following a fall while taking a practice jump on Harris Hill. The *New York Times* reported on the event: "A fatal injury in ski jumping is a rarity—the sport is considered safer than Alpine skiing....Wright's unusual spill, it was felt, stemmed from an airborne posture in which he allowed more air pressure to get under one ski than under the other."[296]

After many years of improvements, including the addition of snowmaking at the ski jumping facility in 1986,[297] the jump went dormant between 2006 and 2008.[298] In 2008, however, the hill was rebuilt. Constructed to conform to International Ski Federation (FIS) standards, it was reprofiled as an 88-meter jump and began holding international FIS competitions.[299] The new hill included a steel tower with new starts and inrun. The landing hill was widened, deflection boards were added to the landing hill and new steel stairs were built going up the side of the landing hill. Since the reconstruction, the annual ski jumping tournament has only grown again in popularity—in 2009, 5,400 spectators attended the jumps, the biggest crowd since 1987, and 18 media outlets came to cover the jumping event. In 2017, a new hill record was set at 104 meters by Blaz Pavlik, an 18-year-old from Slovenia.[300]

In 2019, a new eighteen-meter ski jump with steel tracks was built in Brattleboro, away from Harris Hill but right next to a small ski hill called Living Memorial Park Snow Sports. In 2020, Harris Hill Nordic held its first tournament on the new jump with competitors from all over the Northeast. With this new hill, coach Todd Einig has reintroduced a junior ski jumping program to the town of Brattleboro.

DORMANT JUMPS

MASSACHUSETTS

Williamstown | Williams College (Berlin Mountain)

Ski jumping at Williams College in Williamstown, Massachusetts, began in 1915 with the establishment of the Williams Outing Club and their first Winter Carnival that year. Athletes competed in cross-country ski and snowshoe races, skijoring and jumping on the small hill. As the *Berkshire Eagle* related, the "big event was won by Frank Hutchinson, Class of 1917, as he leaped 10 meters in the ski jump to edge his nearest competitor by two inches."[301]

The Williams Outing Club (WOC) was officially formed that April with fifty students present, under the leadership of Professor A.H. Licklider. Club fees were fifty cents. In 1924, the WOC joined the Intercollegiate Winter Sports Association and began holding the Winter Carnival at Sheep Hill, the Thunderbolt Trail in Adams, Bee Hill and Stone Hill.[302] In the 1930s, Williams College ski coach Jim Parker oversaw the construction of Sheep Hill's first jump and ski tow.[303] This went a long way to attract students, locals and out-of-towners to the joy of skiing; Winter Carnival events frequently attracted over one thousand spectators. By the late 1950s, however, the college began looking for a new location for the ski area that would provide steeper slopes and better snow conditions for the students.[304]

Coach Ralph Townsend, former Nordic Combined Olympian, took over from Al Trudel in 1950 as ski coach and director of the Outing Club, and he was responsible for scoping out and securing an eighty-acre piece of land on nearby Berlin Mountain as Williams College's new venue for ski jumping and skiing. In 1960, the college broke ground on a ski trail with one thousand feet of vertical drop and two ski jumps, a twenty meter and a forty-five meter, on Berlin Mountain. In 1966, Williams added a one-thousand-foot rope tow to the area, and this new area with its larger and better-designed ski jumps enabled Williams students to greatly improve their skiing skills and performance in intercollegiate competitions.[305] The area was named the Ralph Townsend Ski Area.[306] The larger ski jump was thoughtfully designed in an area with shade all day long, providing better snow conditions, and built into the hill with a natural inrun and landing hill.[307]

In the early 1970s, Townsend set up a snowmaking system for the ski area and ski jumps; the Outing Club dug a pond for water, and the Williamstown Fire Department provided one thousand feet of hose to connect the water supply to the snowmaking equipment. Townsend retired in 1972 but remained the director of the Outing Club.[308]

In the 1970s, the ski area suffered due to a lack of more efficient lifts, a snowmaking system that was not sufficient and access to other ski facilities that surpassed Berlin Mountain's range of terrain, and in February 1977, Williams College held the Winter Carnival at Berlin Mountain for the last time.[309] The carnival continued, but Berlin Mountain and its jumps were only used until 1980, when the NCAA dropped ski jumping as a college sport, marking the end of jumping at Williams College.[310]

Today, the jumps and ski trails at Berlin Mountain are mostly overgrown with evergreens, but the profile of the jump can still be seen through the trees.[311] The area is now owned by several organizations, including Williams College, Williamstown, the Massachusetts Department of Conservation & Recreation, the New York Department of Environmental Conservation, Williamstown Rural Lands Foundation and the Berkshire Natural Resources Council, as well as three private landowners, and it has largely been left to nature. Williams College students have stated that they would like to fix up the land by cutting new trails and marking existing ones better, which would make it accessible to more skiers, mountain bikers and hikers. The parking lot for the old ski area would become a trail hub for the college and community.[312]

Bolton | (Norseman's Hill)

In 1950, ski jumping came to the town of Bolton, Massachusetts. The idea for a ski jump and ski hill in town belonged to a man named Donald Erickson, son of Swedish immigrants and an avid ski jumper since the 1920s. In 1948, Erickson bought a one-hundred-acre tract of land at the corner of Route 110 and Route 117 and began clearing the land for what would be three downhill slopes, a toboggan run and a ski jump.[313]

With the help of friends and family members, Erickson built a forty-meter ski jump[314] using lumber cleared from the land and milled at Bud Zink's Saw Mill in town. He also installed a simple rope tow powered by a Ford truck engine and designed a rudimentary snowmaking system to snow the jump. He called his ski area and jump Norseman's Hill.[315]

Competition on Norseman's Hill, Bolton, 1950s. *Courtesy of the Estano family.*

Norseman's Hill, Bolton, 1950s. *Courtesy of the Estano family.*

Quickly, enthusiasm in Bolton grew for the new ski area, and the Bolton Ski Club was formed, which was later sanctioned by the U.S. Eastern Amateur Ski Association. One enthusiastic supporter was Norwegian American ski jumper Strand Mikkelson from Worcester, Massachusetts.[316] The area hosted several ski jumping tournaments, which attracted large crowds.[317] In a presentation on early New England ski jumps, Richard Kenyon quipped, "Skiers sometimes ran out of hill and went across Route 117. They had a flag man who stopped traffic on the road until the skier made his run."[318]

Despite the burst of enthusiasm for Norseman's Hill in the early 1950s, the area closed for good in 1957 due to several warm winters and a lack of snow.[319] Today, the land that was once Norseman's Hill is owned by Bolton Orchards.[320]

New Boston | New England Ski Club (Suicide Hill)

Just off Route 8 in the New Boston hamlet of Sandisfield, Massachusetts, there was once a large ski jump called Suicide Hill. Inspiration for the construction of the ski jump came from the 1932 Lake Placid Olympics, where ski jumping was featured prominently as the most exciting winter sport.[321] Of the new enthusiasm for the sport in New England, the *Sandisfield Times* remembered, "Jumps were built all over the region to lure the stars to perform and enthrall visitors. One of the largest and most spectacular was built in Sandisfield."[322]

Several businessmen from Winsted, a nearby town in Connecticut, invested $7,000 into the building of the jump, designed by Karl Thomlevold for the New England Ski Club.[323] That winter on January 26, 1936, Suicide Hill held an inaugural exhibition jump in front of a crowd of four thousand spectators.[324] Ten Scandinavian American ski jumpers were invited to participate, including female jumper Johanne Kolstad.[325] Many of the jumps ended in crashes, and nobody jumped as far as expected.[326]

The name Suicide Hill perhaps stemmed from the way the particular jump was situated; the *Sandisfield Times* recalled it had a "precipitous eastern face that ran directly down towards Rte 8 and the Farmington River. The take-off point was 425 feet up and the run was 1050 feet long—with a dangerously short landing zone, which helped lure some 4,000 spectators to come to watch those skiers who dared attempt it."[327]

Suicide Hill, 1930s. *Sandisfield Historical Society.*

By the late 1930s, Suicide Hill was struggling due to a few winters with too little snow, and by the early 1940s, the jump had been abandoned and was eventually dismantled.[328] All that is left of Suicide Hill is a barely visible berm and rusting iron to the south of the pizza restaurant Villa Mia, which has since closed.[329]

VERMONT

Middlebury | Middlebury College (Middlebury College Snow Bowl, Chipman Hill)

The Edward Gignac Memorial fifty-five-meter Ski Jump at the Middlebury College Snow Bowl was one of the largest college ski jumps in the nation and an important stop on the NCAA college circuit. The Snow Bowl, one of the earliest ski areas in Vermont, is still in operation and was established by Middlebury College. Ski jumping was featured in the College's Winter Carnivals every year, and in 1961 and 1973, the NCAA College Ski Championships were held at the Snow Bowl and ski jump.[330]

Ski jumping at Middlebury started in 1924 at Chipman Hill Park, just north of campus off Route 7. The first Middlebury jump was roughly a twenty-meter hill and completed just in time for the Middlebury College Winter Carnival that February.[331] In the early 1930s, the college also began to cut ski trails on Worth Mountain, fifteen miles east from the college, an area that would become the Bread Loaf Snow Bowl and finally the Middlebury College Snow Bowl.[332]

By February 1934, Middlebury College students had begun working on a new ski jump near the Chipman Hill slalom course. Funds for the new jump came from the Federal Emergency Relief Administration, established by President Roosevelt to alleviate unemployment at the end of the Great Depression. The new forty-meter hill was patterned after the smaller jumps in Lake Placid, with a thirty-five-foot wooden tower on concrete piers. The jump was completed the following year along with a toboggan and a bobsled run as well as new downhill and slalom courses, all to be used in the Winter Carnivals.[333]

From 1935 to 1936, the hill was renovated to extend the landing hill and outrun areas, and the following year, a fifteen-meter ski jump was constructed to replace the original twenty-meter built in 1924, referred to as the "High School Jump." In 1945, the larger jump at Chipman Hill was replaced with a better designed forty-meter hill which was used for competition only through the 1947 Winter Carnival. The reason for the new jump's short life was a big new project taken on by Middlebury College in the form of a large ski jump at the Middlebury College Snow Bowl,[334] an area which had quickly evolved into a skiing hub for Vermont and New England: a 1949 *New York Times* article referred to the ski area as "one of the most compact and comprehensive collegiate ski layouts in the country…where the snows

Middlebury College ski jump, 1930s or 1940s. *Warren Chivers Archive.*

come frequently and remain long, the Bowl contains just about everything that a skier would enjoy."[335]

In 1946, new trails were cut and a rope tow installed at the Snow Bowl, and the next year the giant fifty-five-meter Edward Gignac Memorial Ski Jump was constructed.[336] A 1947 article in Middlebury's *The Campus* announced:

> *The final finishing touches were made the first part of December to the nation's highest and largest collegiate jump situated in the heart of the College's Bread Loaf Mountain Snow Bowl. The 55 meter jump was officially opened with the first jump being made by Coach Bobo Sheehan, pre-war captain of the Middlebury ski team who returned from World War II naval duty last winter to coach Middlebury College to the 1947 Intercollegiate Ski Union Championship title....The jump has a Northern exposure with a three-quarters natural slope and is located in an area where tests show that "jumping-type" snow remains from early fall to late spring.*[337]

In 1954, a Poma lift was installed, replacing the rope tow. Over the next several years, more trails were cut, and eventually another Poma lift installed in 1963. (It was later replaced by a chairlift in 1984.) In 1969, a smaller forty-meter ski jump was also built to aid in training.[338]

The Gignac Jump, like many other college ski jumps, stopped being used shortly after the NCAA dropped ski jumping as a sanctioned college sport, and the jump was taken down in the late 1980s.[339] The Middlebury College Snow Bowl, however, is still in operation, and serves the Middlebury College ski team training slopes. With three chair lifts that provide access to seventeen trails and gladed areas, the Snow Bowl has come a long way since its beginning. Its long history, however, can still be felt in the heat emitted by the ski area's original fieldstone fireplace, which the base lodge was built around, "where intrepid skiers warmed their woolies in the early days before the lodge was built."[340]

Northfield | Norwich University (Goodrich Ski Area)

Norwich University in Northfield once had a forty-five-meter ski jump as well as a good-sized ski area available to the university students. The jump, built in the early 1920s by the class of 1923, predates the area's ski tows by more than a decade.[341] An electric rope tow was first installed on South

Samples Hill, 1980s. *Warren Chivers Archive.*

Jumper over the town of Norwich, likely by Roger Conant, 1963. *Norwich University Archives, Northfield, Vermont.*

Samples Hill, 1980s. *Warren Chivers Archive.*

Main Street by the Northfield Ski Club in 1936. The tow was purchased for the University in 1939 by William Lybrand, who later donated funds to expand the skiing terrain. In 1961, a gift of land to the university by George Goodrich enabled the ski area to expand, and a hut was built. At this point, the Lybrand Ski area was renamed the Goodrich Ski Area. In 1970, the ski area put in a double chairlift, replacing a Poma lift, and opened to the general public.[342]

In addition to the forty-five-meter jump, there was also a smaller one for younger jumpers and beginners. Former ski jumper Walter Malmquist remembered the jump: "The hill behind the main street in Norwich—there were alpine slopes that the Norwich kids used to walk up—they packed it and skied down, and right next to that hill was the Samples ski jump which was a K15 meter."

By the 1980s and early 1990s, the area was struggling financially. Though it was one of the largest on-campus ski areas in the country, it did not draw many out-of-state visitors, and without snowmaking, low-snow winters threatened the area's viability. After the 1991–92 season, the ski area finally shut down.[343]

Rochester | (Rochester Tow)

SKI JUMPING ON EATON'S HILL 1935

Rochester ski jump, 1935.
Rochester Historical Society.

Rochester, Vermont, was once home to a 70-meter ski jump at a small ski area called the Rochester Tow, located a couple miles north of town off Route 100. The jump was called Eaton's Hill and was situated on land that had been cleared to fuel a local iron furnace in the mid-1800s. The takeoff was built on a rock outcropping shaped perfectly for the purpose. The tow itself was a 1,200-foot apparatus.[344] Jumpers used the hill until 1969, when the surrounding ski area, the Rochester Tow, closed down. Though the jump itself is long gone, the rock outcropping is still visible.[345]

NEW HAMPSHIRE

Hanover | Dartmouth College ("Vale de Tempe")

From the 1920s to 1993, the fifty-meter ski jump at Dartmouth College in Hanover, referred to as the Vale de Tempe jump and situated by the Hanover Country Club's thirteenth green, was a significant jump in the eastern and college circuits. It was also important symbolically for the Dartmouth community, as *The Dartmouth* pointed out, "For generations of college students, the jump—sometimes referred to by its location, the Vale of Tempe—symbolized the outdoor side of Dartmouth."[346] Dartmouth was the first college to incorporate ski jumping into its winter programs, starting in 1911 with the first Winter Carnival. In 1922, the fifty-meter jump was built, and at the time of the jump's dismantling in 1993, Dartmouth was the last college to maintain an active ski jump on campus.[347]

Dartmouth's ski jumping tradition began with the founding of the Dartmouth Outing Club (DOC) in 1909 by Fred Harris, a Dartmouth student and skiing enthusiast from Brattleboro, Vermont. In his junior year, Harris proposed the formation of an outing club in an editorial to the school newspaper. He suggested that the long, cold New Hampshire winters were best taken advantage of by snowshoe and ski trips, and that an end-of-season "Field Day" should occur to give students the opportunity to showcase their new skills.[348] In a 1920 issue of *National Geographic*, Harris wrote: "The fact that Dartmouth College is situated in the sequestered town of Hanover, New Hampshire, among the foothills of the White Mountains, where the hand of winter lies heavy on the land during a large part of the scholastic year, is responsible for the organization of an athletic association unique in the annals of student life in America."[349]

The college liked the idea of an outing club, and in 1911, the winter Field Day proposed by Harris evolved into the first Dartmouth Winter Carnival. To spark interest in the new event and the Outing Club, women were invited to attend the Winter Carnivals, and indoor and outdoor activities were added to the schedule.[350] In the same *National Geographic* article, Harris wrote that ski jumping was

> *the crowning event of the carnival, which is to the occasion what the chariot race of the Olympic games was to the ancients. Thousands of spectators can be accommodated on the slopes surrounding Dartmouth's great ski-jumping course. The approach of the ski-jump is down a steep 300-foot*

pathway cut through a pine forest. At the top is a wooden trestle, which enables the contestant to acquire a tremendous initial momentum for his rush down the course to the "jump" itself, which is a level platform fifty feet long, with a "take-off" eight feet above the slope.[351]

In 1922, the jump was rebuilt as the fifty-meter jump that would last through the decades. Former Dartmouth ski jumper Ted Chivers remembered that "the knoll on the Dartmouth hill was built out of wood, which eventually rotted or was otherwise damaged (possibly from the '38 hurricane) and caved in. Knoll hopping [meaning landing on the knoll] was not recommended, as there remained only a large crater that one had to clear just to stay alive."[352]

In addition to building the ski jump and establishing the Winter Carnival, the DOC also began acquiring and maintaining cabins in the surrounding mountains for use by club members. By the mid-1920s, the DOC was so popular that 73 percent of the student body were members, and by the 1930s, the DOC managed over twenty cabins. The Winter Carnival grew quickly in popularity and was a significant event known throughout the Northeast.[353]

Around 1930, Dartmouth recruited German American Otto Schniebs to coach the school's ski team. The Dartmouth ski team took six national titles under the direction of Coach Schniebs, and in 1936, four students he coached were selected for the U.S. Olympic team.[354] Schniebs coached Dartmouth ski jumpers, including David Bradley, Dick Durrance, Harold Hillman, Eddie "the Snapper" Wells and the Chivers brothers, to national fame. Coach Walter Prager succeeded Schniebs and carried the Dartmouth ski team in its winning streak through the early 1940s. After a period of decreased activity during World War II,[355] ski jumping at Dartmouth returned, and skimeister competitions were increasingly popular.[356]

Jumping at Dartmouth remained strong through the 1960s and 1970s, but a decline began in the early 1980s when the NCAA decided to drop ski jumping from the list of sanctioned college sports. Head ski coach at the time, John Morton, worked hard to keep ski jumping alive at the college, even though the event was no longer part of the college circuit or an official event at the Winter Carnival. Dartmouth continued to hold jumping events and maintain the hill, but eventually the cost of maintenance was too great and a decision was made to tear the jump down in 1993.[357] Ted Chivers recalled the last competition on the great Dartmouth jump: "When word got out that it was due to be demolished, the network of active and former jumpers came alive and a last-minute, informal send-off competition was

The damaged trestle of the Dartmouth jump, possibly taken after the 1938 hurricane. *Warren Chivers Archive.*

The Dartmouth Winter Carnival, 1940s. *Warren Chivers Archive.*

held, marking the last time any of us would ski the 50M hill. We dusted off the skis and up we went—most of us from the picnic table on top to help offset the years and muscle memory loss."[358]

Now, all that remains of the old jump is a granite monument with a bronze plaque that reads:

In memory—
Here stands the grand old Dartmouth Ski Jump
First and last of college big hills
1922 to 1993
98 feet high
35 degrees steep
Hill record 177 feet
"Youth and courage took flight here…
And fired the Carnival air"[359]

NEW YORK

Canton | St. Lawrence University (St. Lawrence Snow Bowl)

For decades, St. Lawrence University (SLU) operated a ski hill called the Snow Bowl, formerly named Cold Creek Valley Ski Hill. In addition to serving as a venue for cross-country and downhill skiing for students from 1938 to 1983, the Snow Bowl held several ski jumps that were part of college jumping tournaments, Winter Carnival events and the New York State Ski Jumping Championships. The Snow Bowl is also known to have been the largest university-run ski area in the country.[360]

SLU skiers first competed at Dartmouth's Winter Carnival events in 1932, marking the beginning of skiing at the college. St. Lawrence established its own yearly winter carnival starting in 1934.[361] While the SLU Ski Team was not officially formed until 1937, skiers initially practiced on a small university-owned hill called Bullis Hill, west of Canton. In the mid-1930s, SLU skiers began scouting out locations for what would be the future Snow Bowl, eventually finding a hillside in South Colton on Route 56 by Cold Brook and working out a lease agreement with the farmer who owned the land. During the summer of 1937, the hillside was cleared, and the first small ski jump was built, and that winter, the Cold Creek Valley Ski Hill opened up for downhill and cross-country skiing, ski jumping and winter

Art Devlin of Lake Placid on the Snow Bowl's forty-six-meter jump, 1951. *St. Lawrence University, Special Collections, Owen D. Young Library.*

carnivals.[362] Otto Schnieb, the well-known ski instructor and former coach from Dartmouth, was hired by St. Lawrence to lead the ski program.[363]

During the 1940s, the college's Winter Carnival featured four days of competitions in cross-country, downhill, slalom and ski jumping, as well as a torchlight parade, hockey, basketball and skijoring. Ski jumping drew in the largest crowds of the events. The carnival concluded with a banquet and a ball for the competitors.[364] In 1943, a rope tow was installed at the ski hill and a larger thirty-meter jump was built, and in 1946 the college purchased the 350-acre piece of land from the farmer, renaming it the Snow Bowl.[365] Along with $19,000 of upgrades to the Snow Bowl over the next two years, the college increased the size of the ski jump to a forty-six-meter jump. In 1952, another jump was built, this time a sixty-meter hill.[366]

At the base of the Snow Bowl, an old barn had been turned into a snack bar, serving hot dogs and burgers, adding to the appeal of spectatorship and creating a popular gathering place for the college.[367] A 1951 *New York Times* described the scene at the Snow Bowl: "Skiing enthusiasm in this college town, always at a high pitch, literally reached the clouds tonight in anticipation of the big-time jump tomorrow on St. Lawrence University's new 60-meter hill."[368]

Rainbow Wright on the Snow Bowl's forty-six-meter jump, 1948. *St. Lawrence University, Special Collections, Owen D. Young Library.*

In 2018, North Country Public Radio interviewed former Snow Bowl manager and ski coach for St. Lawrence, Bob Axtell, then eighty-six: "I remember back in '50, '51, the New York State Jumping Championships were held at the Snow Bowl at that time. We had two outstanding ex-Olympians, Art Devlin and Art Tokle, who jumped. I think the record at that time was 186 feet.…The record when I left was 196 feet.…When we used to practice the jumping, the cars would line up alongside the road just to watch the kids practice.…Then when they had the New York State Championships, those cars were parked just way up as far as you could see, and there were probably 3 or 400 people as spectators watching the jump."[369]

In the early 1970s, however, a few years of too little snowfall forced the college to reconsider the way the Snow Bowl was operating. The university decided to cut back on the ski area's operations and raise ticket prices, but just a few years later, the Snow Bowl again came into question. St. Lawrence was under a tight budget at the time, and the cost to run the Snow Bowl had risen to over $20,000 a year.[370] Decisions on the fate of the Snow Bowl were put off a few years, but by 1982 it was decided that the ski area could no longer operate. In 1983, the area closed forever. This decision was largely a financial one made by the college, but it did not help that the NCAA had cut ski jumping just a couple years before, making the ski jumps useless for the college.[371]

The land became overgrown for the most part, with only remnants of the ski facilities visible here and there. The college continued to use the old Snow Bowl for a school-wide winter party known as the "Snowbowl Extravaganza" with sledding, concerts and big air skiing contests, but in 2004, the college sold the land, marking a true end of an era.[372] North Country Public Radio host Martha Foley acknowledged, "It's pretty much all woods now, and blueberries, but it *used* to be a really state of the art skiing spot in the north country."[373]

Salamanca | Interstate Ski Club (Allegany State Park Ski Jump)

In far Western New York just over an hour south of Buffalo, Allegany State Park was home to two ski jumps—a thirty-meter and a fifty-meter. These were two of the most prominent jumps in Western New York, frequently hosting major ski jumping events from 1935 to 1979. The construction of the jumps was overseen by Art Roscoe and former Olympian Karl Fahner[374] and carried out by the Civilian Conservation Corps. The jumps had well-built stone take-offs that are still standing today.[375]

They were managed by the Allegany State Park's Interstate Ski Club of Red House (ISCRA). From 1894 to 1959, the Red House, a one-room schoolhouse, was located at the base of the ski jumps, and when it closed

The Allegany State Park jumps, still visible in 2013. The fifty meter is on skier's left, the thirty meter is to skier's right. *Courtesy of Jon Nelson.*

in 1959, the ISCRA began to use the old schoolhouse as its clubhouse. The outruns of both jumps had to cross Red House Creek on two different bridges constructed just for that purpose, and the stopping area was just past the creek.[376]

The park held a biannual National Ski Tournament that attracted highly esteemed international jumpers as well as the best national and local jumpers. The first of these tournaments was held on February 24, 1935. More than five thousand people came to watch. As these events were publicized over the years, they drew crowds of up to ten thousand. The 30-meter jump had a hill record of 108 feet, set by local George Boyer in 1948, and the 188-foot hill record on the 50-meter was set by Franz Elsigan of Austria in 1956.[377]

In 1979, the bridges across Red House Creek that were used as part of the jumps' outruns collapsed during a flood, and due to a lack of funding and liability concerns, this event ended ski jumping at Allegany State Park. The last day of jumping at the park was on February 24, 1979.[378]

Bear Mountain | Bear Mountain State Park

Bear Mountain State Park is an hour's drive north of New York City and in the mountainous terrain on the west bank of the Hudson River. Today, visitors to the park can fish and swim in rivers and lakes; hike, bike and cross-country ski on the park's trails; swim in a swimming pool; visit the Trailside Museums and Zoo; and skate on an outdoor rink during the winter.[379] From 1927 to 1990, however, Bear Mountain was also home to a fifty-meter ski jump, an important stop for northeastern jumpers and one that held significant national and international competitions, sometimes drawing crowds of ten to thirty-five thousand spectators.[380] Bear Mountain was one of the premier ski jumping venues in the United States for many years, and it was once in the running to be the site of the 1932 Winter Olympic Games.[381]

Ski jumping competitions held at Bear Mountain were sponsored by a variety of metropolitan area ski clubs and organizations; a January 1982 *New York Times* article lists upcoming competitions and sponsoring clubs:

> *The following tournaments are scheduled at Bear Mountain State Park: Today at 2 P.M.: Telemark Ski Jumping Tournament, sponsored by the Telemark Ski Club. Next Saturday at 2 P.M.: The J.K. McManus Ski Jumping Tournament sponsored by the Bear Mountain Sports Association. Next at 2 P.M.: 61st Anniversary of the Norsemen Ski Jumping Tournament sponsored by the Norsemen Ski Club.*[382]

The park also had a twenty-meter ski jump for children to train on, and in the 1980s, those interested in learning to jump were directed to call the recreation office of the Palisades Interstate Park Commission at Bear Mountain State Park. Former ski jumper Dave Robinson recalled the Bear Mountain jumps:

> *Bear Mountain was 20 miles downriver* [from a ski area in Mt. Beacon, New York] *so we spent quite a bit of time at this state park. Being close to New York City made it great for spectators, but lousy for natural snowfall. So jumps were a continual work in process, with ice shavings from the park's skating rink and gravel-laden "snow" reclaimed from plowed parking lots among the sliding materials we and the park workers applied to the hill. They usually were able to pull off quite a show on the "50 meter" jump most weekends in January and February.*[383]

Bear Mountain, 1935. *Courtesy of Sammlung F.H. and skisprungschanzen.com.*

The Bear Mountain jumps were not an anomaly in the area; at one point in the early twentieth century, the metropolitan area had many ski jumps, thanks to an influx of Norwegian immigrants to the New York City area, especially in Brooklyn. Norwegian communities energized a ski jumping movement in the area, and Bear Mountain was just one of more than nine jumping hills that once dotted the metropolitan landscape. After World War II, jumping activity dropped off, and many of these jumping hills disappeared,[384] but Bear Mountain managed to hang on until 1990, when a decrease in interest in the sport and fewer volunteers made continuing the tradition impossible. Today, the jump is overgrown but still visible.

Rosendale | Rosendale Nordic Ski Club (Joppenbergh Mountain)

The town of Rosendale is located two hours north of New York City in Ulster County and once was home to a seventy-meter ski jump sponsored by the Rosendale Nordic Ski Club. The jump was built on Joppenbergh Mountain, and at one point, it was the club's goal to make Rosendale the "Nordic Ski Capital of the East." Once an important ski jump on the eastern circuit, the site and surrounding land where the jump once was is now overgrown and under the care of the Wallkill Valley Land Trust, used for resource management and habitat restoration.[385]

Joppenbergh Mountain rises up from the Rondout Creek, which flows through town, and is also known as "the Joppenbergh," or "Jacob's Mount," named after Jacobsen Rutger van Schoonderwoerdt, the town's first European settler in 1680. The Joppenbergh is composed of dolostone, which for a long time provided the material necessary to create the water-resistant cement that was the backbone of Rosendale's economy. In 1899, the cement industry in Rosendale failed after the mines collapsed, and the

Rosendale ski jump, 1940s. *The Century House Historical Society.*

Joppenbergh was no longer used for mining dolostone.[386] Though the town's cement industry went under, the unused site of the mines provided a perfect location for a ski jump.

In 1936, a Finnish American named Gus Williams formed the Telemark Ski Club, uniting a group of Scandinavians, mostly Norwegians, to establish skiing in the Rosendale community. They took part in cross-country ski races and built a ski jump at the Joppenbergh the next year,[387] aided by the Rosendale Township Association. The first jump was a 40-meter hill and designed by Harold Schelderup, a Norwegian ski jump designer. The club's goal was to hold its first competition in the winter of 1937, but the weather did not cooperate, and the jump was canceled that first year. Still motivated and determined to pull off an event on the new ski jump, the club rescheduled the inaugural jump to the summer. In July 1937, members covered the hill with pine needles, carpets, straw and Borax to make the jump slippery and held the event in front of 3,300 spectators, during which Ottar Satre from Salisbury Winter Sports Association set the hill record at 112 feet.[388]

The jump was enlarged twice just before the beginning of World War II, from a forty-meter jump to a fifty-meter jump, but competitions stopped during the war and did not resume until the 1960s. In 1964, efforts to revitalize the club and ski jump produced the new Rosendale Nordic Ski Club and the Joppenbergh Mountain Corporation. This entity built a new seventy-meter ski jump in place of the old one, complete with snowmaking and a parking lot with a ten-thousand-car capacity.[389] In 1966, the inaugural competition on the new jump was plagued by too much snow, described in a *New York Times* article:

> *Rosendale, N.Y., Jan. 30—Hard luck was the lot of the Rosendale Nordic Ski Club for the second time this season as a blinding snowstorm prevented it from staging a full-scale jumping tournament today on its new 70-meter hill. Early this month, lack of snow rather than an abundance forced officials of the local club to cancel a meet that was to have brought back competitive jumping here after a lapse of three decades.*[390]

During the last competition in 1971, Middlebury College student Hugh Barber set multiple hill records, jumping in front of a crowd of 3,500.[391] Sadly, jumping was discontinued in Rosendale the next year due to difficulties with funding and inconsistent weather.[392] What is left of the abandoned and overgrown ski jump can still be seen from the trails on Joppenbergh that are available to the public.[393]

Salisbury Mills | Norsemen Ski Club (Norsemen Hill)

Starting in the 1930s in Salisbury Mills, New York, ski jumpers could fly distances of up to sixty meters on Norsemen Hill, a ski jump associated with the Norsemen Ski Club. Local resident Fedela diBenedetto Decker remembered the jump: "It might be hard to imagine now, but Salisbury Mills was once a place where world-class ski jumpers competed in hopes of making it to the Olympics."[394]

Decker remembers that the hill, one of the largest natural jumps in the state at the time, was near the old train trestle in town. Just an hour and a half from New York City, the jump attracted large crowds of spectators who had taken the train in from the city to see the best jumpers compete. *The Photo News* quoted Decker as she recalled participating in hill maintenance with her brother:

We had no money to get in, but my brother Joe and I and the other kids would ski down to Salisbury Mills from Washingtonville and we'd get in for free because they'd use us to pat the snow smooth after each jump. What they did was run a rope from the seating scaffold, then between jumps a few of us would hold onto the rope and ski out onto the hill and use our own skis to pack the snow down where it had been kicked up by the last jumper. They gave us free hot dogs for doing it, too. I saw a skier jump 191 feet there, and I saw a famous Norseman named Torger Tokle jump there, too....I also saw a skier fall and break his neck and die.[395]

International jumpers competed on Norsemen Hill from the 1930s to at least the 1950s. A January 1950 *New York Times* article announced: "The finest brand of ski jumping in the country since the 1932 Winter Olympics at Lake Placid was exhibited today on ice-covered Norsemen Hill, with four Norwegian stars dominating the Federation Internationale de Ski-sanctioned open competition."[396] The *Vassar Chronicle* announcement for the same event read:

Members of the Olympic Ski teams of Norway, Sweden, Finland, Canada and the United States will compete in an international ski tournament to be held at Salisbury Mills, New York tomorrow. This meet which is being sponsored by the Norway Ski Club, the oldest ski club in New York, is quite accessible from Vassar...The tournament, which is sanctioned by S.I.S. and by the National Ski Association, will take place whether there is snow or not, since the hill will be packed with crushed ice. Among the Olympic stars competing will be the Ruud brothers of Norway and Arthur Tokle of the United States. The meet is by invitation of the Metropolitan Ski Jumping Club.[397]

Decker and her brother would cross-country ski five miles from their home to watch ski jumpers on Norsemen Hill. There were smaller jumps nearby, also operated by Norsemen Ski Club, which young jumpers would train on in preparation for the big hill. Decker recalled, "They'd take turns jumping, and then they'd climb the hill sideways with their skis on and do it all over again. When they were done, they'd ski back home to Washingtonville."[398]

The inrun of Norsemen Hill was carved out several feet into the hill, so jumpers skied through a narrow chute with rock or earth walls several feet high before launching off the takeoff of the jump. In a short video put out

Salisbury Mills ski jump, circa 1950.
The Moffat Library.

by *Paramount News* in the 1930s, ski jumpers flew to the bottom of the hill, some landing and some jumps ending in spectacular crashes. The title card of the clip reads "60 M.P.H. On Skis! *Salisbury Mills* N.Y.—Ski artists take chances on most dangerous run in the East! 3,000 brave cold to see Harold Sorenson win amateur title."[399] Abandoned at some point after the 1950s, the jump now exists only in memories and a few photos and videos.

MAINE

Rumford | Chisholm Ski Club (Spruce Street, Scotty's and Black Mountain)

For many decades, Rumford was an important ski jumping venue on the eastern and national circuits. Ski jumping was introduced to Rumford by Scandinavian immigrants who had come to work in the town's paper mills around the turn of the twentieth century. One of these, the Oxford Paper Company, was among a conglomeration of pulp mills developed by Hugh J. Chisholm, an ambitious Canadian industrialist.[400] In 1917, the Rumford Outing Club organized to promote summer and winter activities in the town. A few years later, in 1923, the group reorganized as Chisholm Ski

Club,[401] later renaming itself the Chisholm Skiing and Outing Club and then reverting to Chisholm Ski Club in the 1950s.[402]

Ski jumping became part of life in Rumford when Norwegian immigrant Matthias Nilsen of the Rumford Outing Club helped establish the first ski jump on the edge of town at an old rifle range. This first jump allowed for flights of around forty feet. Jumping soon caught on among the locals, prompting the construction of a larger hill allowing jumps of eighty or ninety feet.[403]

Following the construction of a fifty-meter jump on Spruce Street, the Chisholm Ski Club sponsored Rumford's first Winter Carnival in 1924, featuring skiing, skating and snowshoeing events. Hundreds of spectators from Boston, who had ridden in on "snow trains" to the event, watched as jumpers flew 150 feet on the new jump. The carnival thrived until World War II, during which Chisholm Ski Club activities dwindled, and the tower and the wooden inrun of the jump on Spruce Street collapsed.[404]

After the war, a new fifty-five-meter jump was built, allowing for jumps of up to two hundred feet. Built on a hillside called Scotty's at the edge of town, the area had plenty of open land that could be plowed to accommodate

The Spruce Street ski jump in Rumford, 1930s. *Warren Chivers Archive.*

parked cars. This gave spectators the advantage of being able to watch jumping events from their cars instead of braving the weather.[405] One 1953 *New York Times* article reported on a particularly cold competition day at Scotty's: "The 55-meter incline at Scotts Mountain, four miles out of town, was extremely fast, the hard-frozen granular cover making the riding tricky. Adding to the jumpers' problem was the cold wind that came in blasts. It was one of these blasts that nearly tumbled Blikstad on his second effort."[406]

By 1960, this location was no longer available for use by the Chisholm Ski Club, so the jump was taken down. At this point, the club turned its sights to Black Mountain and the terrain surrounding it for a new recreational complex. Here they built cross-country trails, an alpine ski area as well as three ski jumps at the base: a fifty-meter, a thirty-meter and a twenty-meter.

The alpine ski area is still in operation as Black Mountain of Maine, but the jumps no longer exist due to a lack of support from organizations such as the NCAA. Dennis Breton of the Chisholm Ski Club recalled: "I believe that the first U.S. Women's National Ski Jumping Championship meet in the late '90s was our last jumping competition. In Rumford the jumps were all removed by the year 2000."[407]

Bethel | Gould Academy (Swans Corner Jumps)

Bethel, just south of Sunday River Ski Resort, was once a ski jumping venue with four hills called the Swans Corner Jumps. The jumps and adjacent ski area were established by Gould Academy, a private boarding school, for their ski teams. Prior to the early 1940s, the academy's skiers practiced on a twenty-meter jump on nearby Anderson Hill.[408] Ruel Swain, a 1944 Gould alum, remembered, "Lots of wheelbarrow and shovel work was needed to turn the slope into a ski jump, landing and giant slalom course for high school competition."[409] The jumping venue held ten-meter, twenty-meter, thirty-meter and forty-five-meter jumps, and the area installed a rope tow in 1950,[410] making for much easier access to the ski slopes and the jumps. Thanks to the rope tow, the ski jumps in Bethel experienced a peak in activities in the 1950s.[411] Former ski jumper Robert Remington remembered in *We Jumped*, "The tow line ran up the left side of the thirty-meter jump, powered by a gasoline-powered engine. The rope traveled down the slope along automobile wheels attached to utility poles."[412]

During the 1940s, the Gould Academy Ski Team, coached by Howard Chivers, competed in jumping meets and alpine races against Stephens High

Tom Remington on the Swans Corner Jump in Bethel, circa 1970. Tom's father, Clarence "Rocking Chair" Remington, is poking his head out of the judges stand. "He's pressing out over my skis for me," said Tom. *Courtesy of Tom Remington.*

School in Rumford, Maine; Edward Little High School in Auburn, Maine; and the Berlin, Lebanon and Hanover High Schools in New Hampshire.[413]

Robert Remington fondly remembered the forty-five-meter jump at Swans:

> *The best jump at the Swan's Corner facility was the 45-meter. The sad thing is that it was a jump that didn't get used a lot. It had some design flaws. Two of these flaws could only be overcome by lots of snow and work. The takeoff was too low and it sat too far back from the landing hill. That meant shoveling tons of snow onto the takeoff, building it up to a height that would get us over the knoll and onto the landing hill. If that wasn't enough work, the landing hill had a big sag in it about halfway down and we had to shovel snow into it to get it built up enough to be able to groom the hill into nice shape. The third flaw was easy to deal with. There was no starting tower so we simply hiked back up the slope to a point that would give us the speed we needed. It meant a very long ride on the inrun. It also meant a very long walk to get back to the top for a ride....*

The distance from the end of the take off to the knoll where the landing hill began was longer than normal. When we took off and started to press out over our skis, there was an unusually long delay before the landing slope came into view. But, when it did, what a feeling! There was an extra rush of pressure against the body and skis and we could extend and press out and down the hill.[414]

In the early 1980s, the end of college jumping coupled with two consecutive years of very little snow moved the Maine Principals Association (the governing body in charge of high school athletics in Maine) to drop ski jumping in 1981, and the jumps fell into disuse.[415]

In the mid-1990s, however, jumping returned to Bethel for a few years when the thirty-meter jump was redesigned and rebuilt by volunteers, enabling the Gould Academy Jumping Team to compete around New England once again.[416] But by the early 2000s, the jump closed for good, ending Gould Academy's long history of ski jumping.

Andover | Andover Pineland Ski Club (Andover Airport Jumps)

Starting in the early twentieth century, the Pineland Ski Club in Andover, Maine, promoted ski jumping, hosting annual Winter Carnivals that featured both cross-country skiing and ski jumping, ending with a dance in the evening. Ski jumping was the most popular event at the carnivals in the first half of the century.[417]

Behind the Andover Town Hall there was a twenty-meter ski jump with a trestle for the inrun rising twenty-five feet high. According to Robert Remington in *We Jumped*, "Andover, Maine produced some of the hottest jumpers from around the state and New England and the town hall jump was probably a good reason for it. Kids had easy access to the jump located a short walk from the center of town and they jumped all hours of the day and night."[418]

There were also two jumps located just south of Andover at the base of a mountain in an open field that was cleared during World War II for possible use as an airport.[419] The area featured a twenty-five-meter jump used mostly by the high school and a forty-five-meter jump. Remington recalled that the twenty-five-meter jump "had a natural in-run with a wooden take-off. The design was out-dated; it sent you out and suddenly down, making it difficult to hold a good flight position."[420] The forty-five-meter jump was situated on a hill that naturally provided a good landing hill profile; much of the inrun had been blasted with dynamite out of the one-hundred-foot ledge that stood in its way. The takeoff of the jump was a built wooden structure fifteen feet high and thirty to forty feet long, and there was a judges tower to the side of the landing hill as well as a warming hut at the base of the jump.[421]

There was once an even larger jump at the airport site, Remington remembered:

> *When we stood on the outrun of the 45 meter at the Andover airport and looked toward the mountain, we could see a wide open area to the left that ran well up the side of the mountain. We were always told that that used to be the site of a much larger jump (60+ meters). It was known as "the man-killer." Rumor had it that during its day a man died as a result of injuries from a fall. Anyone who may know the truth has most likely passed….There seems to be little recorded history of that jump or even how it got its nickname.[422]*

The annual Winter Carnival, sponsored by the Pineland Ski Club, was the big event of the year. Due to the amount of effort needed to prepare the forty-five-meter jump, the club usually waited until just before the carnival to get it ready for use.[423] Tom Remington recalled the excitement of the ski jumping events at the carnival, which often included side-by-side jumpers and participants skiing through flaming hoops:

> *The Andover Winter Carnival was one of a few major winter skiing events held in Maine….I remember vividly the nighttime ski jumping exhibition. There were no electric lights on the Andover 45-meter jump, but it didn't matter. A large, flaming hoop, several feet in diameter stood at the end of the takeoff and torches lined the in-run and landing hill. Jumpers willing to risk their necks carried a torch in each hand as they went off the jump. The crowd loved it and showed their appreciation after each jumper with a lengthy "applause" that came from car horns in the parking lot.[424]*

On Sunday of the carnival, the Pineland Ski Club held the Northern New England Ski Jumping Championships; jumpers from all over the Northeast and Canada would compete in the event, and a public address system announced the jumpers' names and distances for the spectators.[425]

Andover Airport jumps: forty-five meter on skier's left with the "Man-Killer" jump to the right, 1959. *Courtesy of Mike Stowell.*

The forty-five-meter jump at the airport was used into the early 1960s, and the larger "Man-Killer" jump stopped being used after World War II. Smaller jumps in town were used for youth jumping into the 1980s, but after that, there was no more ski jumping in Andover.[426] More recently, the Pineland Ski Club has focused on ski programs for the Andover Elementary School, and groomed cross-country ski trails are maintained by the Akers family and available for club and community use.[427]

CONNECTICUT

Norfolk | Norfolk Winter Sports Association

There was a burst of skiing enthusiasm in Norfolk in the 1930s when several local and Scandinavian American skiers and ski jumpers—including Harold Sorenson, Birger Torrissen, Olle Zetterstrom and the Hegge brothers—decided to form the Norfolk Winter Sports Association (NWSA). The group cut ski trails in the mountains by Route 44 (Canaan Road) and conducted ski lessons for adults and children. In 1932, a forty-five-meter ski jump was built on the side of Canaan Mountain.[428]

The jump, built by John Mulville with the help of Birger Torrissen, who designed the hill, had no trestle or tower and was completely built into the hill. Its inaugural competition was held the following winter in February 1933, and afterward the Norfolk Winter Sports Association held amateur competitions on the jump each year until 1938.[429] Norfolk was briefly known as the winter sports center of the state, attracting some of the country's best ski jumpers to the competitions.[430] A much smaller jump was also constructed in 1933 for developing young jumpers. In 1935, Norfolk even

Norfolk ski jump, 1930s. *The Norfolk Historical Society.*

held a summertime meet on the ski jump, covering the hill with pine needles to allow the skis to slide.[431]

Snow trains from New York City stopped in Canaan, near Norfolk, for passengers to make use of the ski trails and watch skiers fly off the jump. In 1935, two Norfolk ski jumpers, Birger Torrissen and Nils Beckstrom, made the U.S. Olympic team for jumping and cross-country skiing and headed to the 1936 Olympic Games in Garmisch-Partenkirchen, Germany.[432]

The last competition on the Norfolk jump was held in 1938. Warm weather and rain threatened to ruin the event, but secretary of the NWSA Mrs. R. Graham Bigelow arranged to have the ice pulverizing machine (likely used for the Winter Carnivals in Madison Square Garden) brought to Norfolk from New York City to save the day. As recalled in *Norfolk, Connecticut 1900–1975*, with the ice machine in place, "a fleet of trucks began to haul cakes of ice from Twin Lakes to the bottom of the hill. The crushed ice then had to be packed on the hill and on the take-off to a depth of six inches."[433] The competition went off smoothly with forty skiers and two thousand spectators, but with that competition, ski jumping in Norfolk had come to a close forever. The trails are still actively used in town for cross-country skiing.[434]

Colebrook | (Colebrook River Ski Hill)

During the 1930s and early '40s, there was a ski jump in Colebrook, a town in northwestern Connecticut right on the Massachusetts line. The fifty-meter jump was located on the eastern side of Spencer Mountain.

Colebrook ski jump, 1930s. *The Norfolk Historical Society.*

Strand Mikkelsen flies off the Colebrook jump, 1930s. *Courtesy of Jim Cormier.*

The hill was designed by Anton Lekang[435] and built by Ralph Strand in the early 1930s. On its opening competition day, it caused a huge traffic jam,[436] which, according to Bob Grigg of the Colebrook Historical Society, was the "worst traffic tie-up ever to occur in the state, caus(ing) cars to be backed up as far south as Thomaston,"[437] which is several towns south of Colebrook.[438] The event was attended by the Norwegian consulate, and tickets sold for five dollars.[439]

Colebrook resident Charles Everett recalled, "That certainly was some hill in Colebrook river. I walked up the stairs one day to the top. How anyone could ski down that hill was unbelievable."[440] Unfortunately, by 1944 the jump proved to be unsuccessful financially and was closed down.[441]

APPENDIX

ACTIVE CLUBS AND HILLS

Club/Hill	<K15	K15-K20	~K25	~K30	~K35	~K50	~K65	~K90
NEW HAMPSHIRE								
Andover Outing Club/Proctor Academy (Blackwater Ski Area)	x	x		x	x			
Hanover High/ Ford Sayre (Oak Hill, Roger Burt Memorial Ski Jumps)	x		x		x			
Conway/Mount Washington Valley Ski Jumping/ Kennett High School	x			x				
Gilford/Gunstock Nordic Association	x	x						
Newport/ Kearsarge/Sunapee	x	x			x			
Plymouth High (Bobcat Hill)		x		x				

Club/Hill	<K15	K15-K20	~K25	~K30	~K35	~K50	~K65	~K90
Lebanon Outing Club (Storrs Hill/ Heistad Hill)	x		x			x		
NEW YORK								
Lake Placid/NYSEF		x				x		x
CONNECTICUT								
Salisbury Winter Sports Association (Satre Hill)		x		x			x	
VERMONT								
Brattleboro/ Harris Hill Nordic (Harris Hill)								x
Brattleboro/ Harris Hill Nordic (Memorial Park)	x	x						

FORMER CLUBS AND HILLS*

Club/Hill	<K15	K15-K20	~K25	~K30	~K35	~K50	~K65	~K90
MASSACHUSETTS								
Andover/Phillips Academy (Holt Hill)		x						
Deerfield/Deerfield Academy		x			x			
Williams College (Berlin Mountain)		x				x		
Williamstown (Sheep Hill)		x						
Greenfield				x				
Groton (Priest's Hills/Carlisle)	x		x					
Lancaster					x			
Pittsfield (Bear Town State Forest)				x				

Club/Hill	<K15	K15-K20	~K25	~K30	~K35	~K50	~K65	~K90
Quincy (Blue Hills)					x			
Bolton (Norseman's Hill)						x		
Ayer (Ski Pingry Hill)						x		
New Boston (Suicide Hill)						x		
VERMONT								
Saxtons River/ Vermont Academy	x		x		x			
Barre		x						
Bradford/Oxbow High School		x	x					
Brattleboro (Latchis Hill)				x				
Burlington (Centennial Park)		x						
Montpelier/ Vermont College (Sabin's Pasture)					x			
Lyndonville/ Lyndonville Outing Club		x	x					
Lyndonville (Shonya Hill)					x			
Lyndonville/ Lyndonville Outing Club (Lybran Trail)				x				
Dummerston (Maple Valley Ski Area)					x			
Middlebury/ Middlebury College Snow Bowl (Chipman Hill)		x			x		x	
Newport				x				
Northfield/Norwich University				x		x		
Norwich (Samples Hill)		x						

137

Club/Hill	<K15	K15-K20	~K25	~K30	~K35	~K50	~K65	~K90
Putney School (Elm Lea Farm Ski Jump)			x					
Rochester						x		
St. Albans		x						
Stowe (Marshall Hill)		x						
Thetford Center (Gus Jacacci Hill)			x					
Williston		x			x			
Woodford (Prospect Mountain)			x					
NEW HAMPSHIRE								
Berlin ("Nansen")		x			x			x
Berlin (12th Street Bridge/Paine's Hill Pasture)					x			
Canaan/Cardigan Mountain School		x						
Concord (Russell Pond/Penacook Lake Ski Jump)			x					
Franconia (Cannon Mountain)		x		x		x		
Gilford (Gunstock)		x			x			x
Hanover/Dartmouth College		x			x			
Henniker/New England College					x			
Holderness School		x			x			
Meriden (KUA Ski Hill)		x		x		x		
New London (King's Ridge)		x						
New Hampton School	Hill size unknown							
Tilton School	Hill size unknown							

Club/Hill	<K15	K15-K20	~K25	~K30	~K35	~K50	~K65	~K90
New York								
Canton/St. Lawrence University (South Colton Snow Bowl)		x			x		x	
Canton/St. Lawrence University (Little River Snow Bowl)			x		x	x		
Salamanca (Allegany State Park Ski Jump)				x		x		
Central Park		x						
Bear Mountain State Park		x				x		
North Creek (Gore Mountain)	Hill size unknown							
Ithaca/Cornell University				x				
Lake Placid (Arena)		x		x				
Lake Placid (Golf Club)			x					
Mount Beacon		x		x				
Newburgh	Hill size unknown							
Old Forge (Maple Ridge)	x	x			x			
Glens Falls (West Mountain)				x				
Glenwood (Glenwood Acres)		x	x					
Rosendale		x			x		x	
Rochester			x		x		x	
Salisbury Mills (Norsemen's Ski Hill)					x			
Saranac Lake (Blood Hill)					x			
Tupper Lake	Hill size unknown							

Club/Hill	<K15	K15-K20	~K25	~K30	~K35	~K50	~K65	~K90
West Harrison/ Norway Ski Club (Silver Lake/St Mary's Lake)					x			
West Lebanon/Sons of Norway	Hill size unknown							
White Plains (Norway Ski Hill)					x			
Milbrook School	Hill size unknown							
MAINE								
Rumford (Black Mountain)		x	x		x		x	
Rumford (Scotty's Mountain)			x	x			x	
Bethel/Gould Academy (Swans Corner)	x	x		x		x		
Cumberland/New Gloucester High School (Hurricane Mt., Gray)	Hill size unknown							
Andover (Aker's/ Elm Street Jump)	x	x						
Andover (Airport Jumps)			x			x	x	
Hebron Academy	Hill size unknown							
Lewiston/Auburn/ Bates College (Pettengil Park)				x				
Livermore Falls				x				
Farmington/ University of Maine Farmington (Titcomb Mt.)	x		x					
Fryeburg (Starks)	Hill size unknown							
Kents Hill	Hill size unknown							
Oxford Hills High School	Hill size unknown							

Club/Hill	<K15	K15-K20	~K25	~K30	~K35	~K50	~K65	~K90
Portland (West Promenade Winter Carnival)				x				
Waterville/Colby College				x				
CONNECTICUT								
Salisbury School		x						
Lakeville/Indian Mountain School		x						
Salisbury/Hotchkiss School		x						
Taconic		x						
Salisbury/ Undermountain Road		x						
Norfolk						x		
Canaan/Salisbury Road/Byrd Ski Club		x						
Canaan/Granite Ave./Byrd Ski Club	x							
Canton	Hill size unknown							
Colebrook (Colebrook River Ski Hill)						x		
Sharon	Hill size unknown							
PENNSYLVANIA								
Analomink (Alpine Mtn)			x					
Canadensis/ Henryville (Timber Hill/Alpine Mountain Ski Resort)				x				
Penn State (Skimont/Tussey Mt)	Hill size unknown							
NEW JERSEY								
McAfee (Great Gorge North)				x				

Club/Hill	<K15	K15-K20	~K25	~K30	~K35	~K50	~K65	~K90
Bedminster/Peapack		x						
Newfoundland/ Odin Ski Club (Craigmeur Ski Area)			x					
Sussex (High Point State Park)				x				
Lake Telemark/ Odin Ski Club	x			x				
Paterson/Swedish Ski Club (North Jersey Country Club)	Hill size unknown							

By Walter Malmquist (a work in progress)

NOTES

1. Introduction

1. Malmquist, email, February 3, 2020.
2. Gasser, "Jumping Hills Construction."
3. Picton, interview.
4. Malmquist, interview.
5. Gasser, "Jumping Hills Construction."
6. Ibid.
7. Ibid.

2. A Norwegian Sport Takes Flight

8. Huntford, *Two Planks*, 2.
9. Bays, *Nine Thousand Years of Skis*, 20.
10. Denning, *Skiing into Modernity*, 31.
11. Bays, *Nine Thousand Years of Skis*, 26.
12. Huntford, *Two Planks*, 4.
13. Ibid., 5.
14. Rybczynski, *Clearing in the Distance*, 271.
15. National Park Service, "Yellowstone: History and Culture."
16. National Park Service, "Quick History."
17. Hanson, "Recreation Movement."

18. Waterman and Waterman, *Forest and Crag*, 183.
19. Ibid., 191.
20. Ibid., 540.
21. Ashburner, *History of Ski Jumping*, 11.
22. Anson, *Jumping Through Time*, 18.
23. Ibid, 19.
24. Huntford, *Two Planks*, 83.
25. Ashburner, *History of Ski Jumping*, 23.
26. Anson, *Jumping Through Time*, 20.
27. Allen, *From Skisport to Skiing*, 11.
28. Ibid., 47.
29. Kobak, "No Man Is a Hero."
30. Huntford, *Two Planks*, 155.
31. Fry, *Story of Modern Skiing*, 5.
32. Bays, *Nine Thousand Years of Skis*, 76.
33. Allen, *From Skisport to Skiing*, 17.
34. Ashburner, *History of Ski Jumping*, 23.
35. Fry, *Story of Modern Skiing*, 9.
36. Cayton, Gorn and William, *Encyclopedia of American Social History*, 703–5.
37. Ibid.
38. Ibid.
39. Anson, *Jumping Through Time*, 22–27.
40. Ibid., 62–64.
41. Ibid., 65, 69.
42. "Norwegians of Bay Ridge, a Proud and Tight-Knit Community," *New York Times*, May 16, 1971.
43. Dechillo, "Ski Jumping Faces Long Decline," 2.
44. Anson, *Jumping Through Time*, 71–88.
45. Grabel, "County Was a Ski-Jump Destination."
46. Dechillo, "Ski Jumping Faces Long Decline," 2.
47. Anson, *Jumping Through Time*, 80.
48. Sprague, "History Timeline."
49. Anson, *Jumping Through Time*, 83; Ski Jumping Hill Archive, "Bethel."
50. Pennington, "Ski Report."
51. Anson, *Jumping Through Time*, 81.
52. Ibid., 71.
53. Waldecker, *Norfolk, Connecticut 1900–1975*, 228.
54. Davis, "Sharon Mountain Ski Area."
55. Davis, *Lost Ski Areas*, 111, 120, 219.

56. Ski Jumping Hill Archive, "Massachusetts."
57. Butynski, "Jaywalking."
58. Colorado Ski History, "Colorado Ski History Timeline 1900–1919."
59. "Dartmouth's Big Carnival," *New York Times*, February 12, 1916.
60. Allen, *From Skisport to Skiing*, 106.
61. "250 On Special Ski Train," *New York Times*, December 27, 1938.
62. Davis, *Lost Ski Areas*, 15.
63. Fry, *Story of Modern Skiing*, 7.
64. Elkins, "Ski Curtain Rises."
65. Lund, "The 1930s."
66. New England Ski History, "Stowe Mountain Resort."
67. Thibault, "This Place in History."
68. Lund, "The 1930s."
69. Erwin, "Salisbury, Connecticut's Jumpfest 2015."
70. Given, "Salisbury."
71. Dechillo, "Ski Jumping Faces Long Decline," 1.
72. Annette R. Hofmann and Gerd Von Der Lippe, "European Pioneers of Women's Ski Jumping: The 'Floating Baroness' from Austria and Norway's 'Queen of Skis'" in *License to Jump! A Story of Women's Ski Jumping*, ed. Marit Stub Nybelius and Annette R. Hofmann (Falun, Sweden: Scandbook, 2015), 25.
73. Ibid., 26.
74. Hinkley and Hastings, "US Athlete Participation 2018/19."

3. A Dwindling American Sport

75. Calamur, "Why Norwegians Aren't Moving."
76. Ibid.
77. Ibid.
78. Dechillo, "Ski Jumping Faces Long Decline."
79. Malmquist, email and "Eastern Jumps" spreadsheet, April 5, 2020.
80. Levasseur, interview, December 21, 2019.
81. Heistad, interview, February 17, 2020.
82. Tokle, interview, February 25, 2020.
83. Stone, interview, March 3, 2020.
84. Malmquist, telephone interview, February 4, 2020.
85. Levasseur, interview, December 21, 2019.
86. Schutz, "'Olympic Village' of Nyack."

87. Heistad, interview, February 17, 2020.

88. Miller, "Jim McKay."

89. Ibid.

90. Malmquist, telephone interview, February 4, 2020.

91. Heistad, interview, February 17, 2020.

92. Jones, interview, January 31, 2020.

93. Gildea, "Dartmouth and the Debate."

94. Stone, interview, March 3, 2020.

95. Tokle, interview, February 25, 2020.

96. Heistad, interview, February 17, 2020.

97. "Summaries of Lake Placid Events," *New York Times*, January 2, 1938, accessed March 1, 2020, https://www.nytimes.com/1938/01/02/archives/summaries-of-lake-placid-events-ski-jumping-combined-ski-event.html; Jay Burns, "Video: Watch Ski Jumping off Mount David in 1936," Bates, February 21, 2018, accessed February 28, 2020, https://www.bates.edu/news/2018/02/21/video-ski-jumping-off-mount-david-in-the-1930s/.

98. Levasseur, interview, December 21, 2019.

99 Josh Fischel, "In Winter, Only in New Hampshire," *New York Times*, February 16, 2012, accessed March 1, 2020, https://www.nytimes.com/2012/02/17/sports/in-new-hampshire-high-school-ski-jumping-still-flies.html.

100 Fischel, "In Winter, Only in New Hampshire."

101. Malmquist, telephone interview, February 4, 2020.

102. Ibid.

103. Jones, interview, January 31, 2020.

104. Malmquist, telephone interview, February 4, 2020.

105 William N. Wallace, "Coucheron Gains Ski-Jumping Title," *New York Times*, February 11, 1968, accessed February 25, 2020, https://www.nytimes.com/1968/02/11/archives/coucheron-gains-skijumping-title-norwegian-paces-dartmouth-to.html.

106. Malmquist, telephone interview, February 4, 2020.

107. Gildea, "Dartmouth and the Debate," 288.

108. Ibid.

109. Heistad, interview, February 17, 2020.

110. Stone, interview, March 3, 2020.

111. Gildea, "Dartmouth and the Debate," 286.

112. "Skimeister," Merriam-Webster Dictionary, https://www.merriam-webster.com/ dictionary/skimeister.

113. "Dartmouth Takes Eastern Ski Title," *New York Times*, February 25, 1968.
114. Allen, *Historical Dictionary of Skiing*, 178.
115. Heath, "Winter Sports Legacy."
116. Heistad, interview, February 17, 2020.
117. Malmquist, telephone interview, February 4, 2020.
118. Ibid.
119. Koenig, "Cross-Country Ski Craze."
120. Malmquist, telephone interview, February 4, 2020.
121. Malmquist, email, February 3, 2020.
122. Malmquist, telephone interview, February 4, 2020.
123. Fiertz, interview, February 1, 2020.
124. Mark Picton, interview, February 3, 2020.
125. Ibid.
126. Ibid.

4. The Power of Community: Ski Jumping's Success in the Northeast

127. "Ski Jumping," Olympic Games, https://www.olympic.org/ski-jumping.
128. "Winter Games," Olympic Games, https://www.olympic.org/winter-games.
129. Pegler, "Olympic Winter Games Open Today."
130. "Lake Placid Awaits Rain, Cold Needed for Winter Olympics," *Washington Post*, January 16, 1932.
131. "Normal Hill Individual Men," Olympic Games, https://www.olympic.org/chamonix-1924/ski-jumping/normal-hill-individual-men.
132. "Nordic Combined," Olympic Games, https://www.olympic.org/vancouver-2010/nordic-combined.
133. Belson, "US In Nordic Combined."
134. Thomas, "After Long Fight for Inclusion."
135. Zinser, "American Wins Women's World Title."
136. *Ready to Fly*, directed by William Kerig.
137. Rosin, "Their Rejection, Our Loss."
138. Macarthur, "Taking Flight."
139. Stone, interview, March 3, 2020.
140. Ibid.
141. Rosin, "Their Rejection, Our Loss."

142. "Our Olympic Story," Women's Ski Jumping USA, http://www.wsjusa. com/olympic-inclusion.

143. Ibid.

144. *Ready to Fly.*

145. Thomas, "After Long Fight for Inclusion."

146. Rosin, "Their Rejection, Our Loss."

147. *Ready to Fly.*

148. Thomas, "After Long Fight for Inclusion."

149. *Ready to Fly.*

150. Stone, interview, March 3, 2020.

151. Gibson, "Sochi 2014."

152. Rosin, "Their Rejection, Our Loss."

153. *Ready to Fly.*

154. Gibson, "Sochi 2014."

155. "Salisbury Invitational Ski Jumping," Jumpfest, http://www.jumpfest.org/.

156. Branch, "It Seems Ski Jumping Has Become a Picnic."

157. "Photos: The Hill Came Alive," *Bennington Banner*, February 17, 2020.

158. Strauss, "Ski Jump Honors Taken By Barber."

159. Brattleboro Reformer Historical Society, "Toboggan Slide Was Part of Winter Attraction."

160. Katharine Erwin, "Salisbury, Connecticut's Jumpfest 2015."

161. Ibid.

162. Riley, "Salisbury's Ski Jumping Tradition Continues."

163. Picton, interview, February 3, 2020.

164. Kiefer, interview, February 12, 2020.

165. Ibid.

166. Erwin, "Salisbury, Connecticut's Jumpfest 2015."

167. Mays, "Ski Jump Event a Family Effort."

168. Kiefer, interview, February 12, 2020.

169. Picton, interview, February 3, 2020.

170. Ibid.

171. Kiefer, interview, February 12, 2020.

172. Ibid.

173. Ibid.

174. "Snow, Ice and Skis at Lake Placid Tomorrow," *New York Times*, July 3, 1956.

175. Heistad, interview, February 17, 2020.

176. Picton, interview, February 3, 2020.

177. Heistad, interview, February 17, 2020.

5. Conclusion

178. Picton, interview, February 3, 2020.
179. Fiertz, "View from the Top."
180. Reid, "Rebuilt by Bow Contractor."
181. Heistad, interview, February 17, 2020.
182. Ibid.
183. Stone, interview, March 3, 2020.
184. Gilbert, "Lessons from My Son."
185. Heistad, interview, February 17, 2020.

Active Jumps
New Hampshire

186. "Ski Jumping at Proctor," Proctor, https://www.proctoracademy.org/on-campus/athletics/proctor-on-snow/ski-jumping.
187. Norris, personal communication, July 8, 2020.
188. Wallen, "Andover's Little League of Skiing," 52.
189. Hinkley, "Legend Retires but the Future Is Bright."
190. Wallen, "Andover's Little League of Skiing," 54.
191. Ibid., 56.
192. Hinkley, "Legend Retires but the Future Is Bright."
193. "Tim Norris," *The Dubliner*, Spring 2018, 36.
194. Hinkley, "Legend Retires but the Future Is Bright."
195. "Oak Hill Hanover, NH," New England Lost Ski Areas Project, http://www.nelsap.org/nh/oakhill.html.
196. "Ford Sayre History," Ford K. Sayre Memorial Ski Council, included in email correspondence between Tom Dodds and author, July 22, 2020.
197. Ibid.
198. Ibid.
199. Burt email to Tom Dodds.
200. "Oak Hill Hanover, NH."
201. Ford Sayre Council letter to George T. Sayre.
202. Ibid.
203. "Ski Jumping," Ford K. Sayre Memorial Ski Council, https://www.fordsayre.org/nordic/jumping/.
204. Allen, *Memoir*, 34.
205. Ibid., 24, 34.

206. Ibid., 35.
207. Ibid., 34.
208. Ibid., 35.
209. Ibid., 30, 36, 39.
210. Ibid., 37.
211. Ibid., 25, 28.
212. Sullivan, "Flying into the Night."
213. Ibid.
214. "Historical Chronology of Newport," Town of Newport, New Hampshire, https://www.newportnh.gov/sites/g/files/vyhlif4776/f/uploads/historical_chronology_story.pdf.
215. "Roland Tremblay Ski Jump Complex," Newport Recreation Department, http://www.newportrec.com/index.php?n=roland_tremblay_ski_jump_complex.
216. "Charles Mallett '41, Roland Tremblay '51 and John Kluge '66," Kimball Union, https://www.kua.org/news-detail?pk=276740.
217. Sullivan, "Flying into the Night."
218. Eastman, "Ski Jumping in the Valley."
219. Ward, "Jump above the Rest."
220. "Making the Jump," *Laconia Daily Sun*, December 11, 2015.
221. Ibid.
222. Boone, "New Hampshire Community Rallies."
223. "Making the Jump."
224. Stepp, "Gene Ross Memorial Ski Jump."
225. "Erling Heistad," US Ski and Snowboard Hall of Fame, https://skihall.com/hall-of-famers/erling-heistad/#:~:text=Erling%20Heistad%20was%20elected%20to,25%20and%2050%20meter%20hills.
226. Heistad, interview, February 17, 2020.
227. Ibid.
228. Ibid.
229. "Erling Heistad."
230. Heistad, interview, February 17, 2020.
231. "Erling Heistad."
232. Heistad, interview, February 17, 2020.
233. Orlowski, "Storrs Hill Ski Area."
234. McPhaul, "Berlin's Nansen Ski Jump."
235. Nadeau, "Nansen Ski Club and Ski Jump."
236. Leich, "Nordic Skiing from Stone Age to Skating."
237. Nadeau, "Nansen Ski Club and Ski Jump."

238. Leich, "Nordic Skiing from Stone Age to Skating," 4.

239. Leich, "Green Mountains, White Gold," 12.

240. "Seek to Aid Ski Jumper under Death Sentence," *New York Times*, March 28, 1930.

241. McPhaul, "Big Nansen," 9.

242. Nadeau, "Nansen Ski Club and Ski Jump."

243. McPhaul, "Big Nansen," 11.

244. Ibid.

245. McPhaul, "Berlin's Nansen Ski Jump."

246. McPhaul, "Big Nansen," 7.

247. Ibid., 14.

248. Ibid., 15.

249. Nadeau, "Nansen Ski Club and Ski Jump."

250. McPhaul, "Big Nansen," 15.

251. "Nansen Ski Club Inc.," NH Gives, https://www.nhgives.org/organizations/nansen-ski-club-inc.

New York

252. "In the Heart of the Adirondacks," *New York Times*, July 9, 1893.

253. "Winter's Splendor in the Adirondacks," *New York Times*, December 17, 1916.

254. Lattimer, *III Olympic Winter Games Lake Placid 1932 Official Report*, 37.

255. Manchester, ed., *Lake Placid Club*, 1–3.

256. "Lake Placid," Ski Jumping Hill Archive, http://www.skisprungschanzen.com/EN/Ski+Jumps/USA-United+States/NY-New+York/Lake+Placid/0576-MacKenzie+Intervale+Ski+Jumping+Complex/.

257. Lattimer, *III Olympic Winter Games Lake Placid 1932 Official Report*, 39.

258. Ibid., 41.

259. Ibid., 142.

260. Ibid., 39.

261. Ibid., 142.

262. Ibid., 142.

263. Ibid., 167.

264. Ibid., 178.

265. "Lake Placid."

266. Strauss, "Kennedy Games at Lake Placid."

267. *Final Report: XIII Olympic Winter Games, Lake Placid, N.Y., February 13–24, 1980*, 38.
268. "Lake Placid."

Connecticut

269. "Ski Jumping Comes to Salisbury," Salisbury Association display panel.
270. Ibid.
271. "Salisbury Is Still Jumping," Salisbury Association display panel.
272. "Satre Takes Title with 152-Foot Leap," *New York Times*, January 26, 1931.
273. "Roy Sherwood 1932–2017," *2018 Salisbury Ski Jumps 92nd Annual Jumpfest Program*.
274. "Roy R. Sherwood," Republican American Archives, https://archives.rep-am.com/2017/10/23/roy-r-sherwood/.
275. Strauss, "Ski-Jumping Won by Roy Sherwood."
276. "Salisbury Is Still Jumping."
277. Elkins, "Norwegian, Canadian and American Squads Compete."
278. "Salisbury Is Still Jumping."
279. Elkins, "Norwegian, Canadian and American Squads Compete."
280. Pennington, "Small Town's Leap of Faith."

Vermont

281. Leich, "Green Mountains, White Gold," 12.
282. Ibid.
283. "Genius, Genesis and Enduring Legacy of Fred Harris," Brattleboro Outing Club, https://brattleborooutingclub.org/wp-content/uploads/2020/04/history1.pdf.
284. Ibid.
285. Leich, "Green Mountains, White Gold," 12.
286. Ibid., 13.
287. Ibid., 12.
288. Ibid., 17.
289. Leich, "Nordic Skiing from Stone Age to Skating," 4.
290. Leich, "Green Mountains, White Gold," 12.
291. "College Ski Title Won by Michelson," *New York Times*, February 15, 1924.
292. Leich, "Nordic Skiing from Stone Age to Skating," 13.

293. Sprague, "History Timeline."
294. "History," Brattleboro Outing Club, https://brattleborooutingclub. org/wp-content/uploads/2020/04/history2.pdf.
295. Sprague, "History Timeline."
296. Strauss, "Fall Kills U.S. Ski Jumper," *New York Times*, January 6, 1975.
297. Sprague, "History Timeline."
298. "History," Brattleboro Outing Club.
299. "Frequently Asked Questions," Harris Hill Ski Jump, https:// harrishillskijump.com/faqs.
300. Sprague, "History Timeline."

Dormant Jumps
Massachusetts

301. Walden, "Williams Carnival Plunges On."
302. Ibid.
303. Slack, "Williams Outing Club."
304. Hunsaker and Kannegieser, "History of Recreational Skiing," 13.
305. Walden, "Williams Carnival Plunges on Despite Paucity of Snow."
306. Hitchcock, "College Racing."
307. "Williams Skiers Try New Jump," *North Adams Transcript*, January 13, 1961.
308. Walden, "Williams Carnival Plunges On."
309. Hunsaker and Kannegieser, "History of Recreational Skiing," 15.
310. Ibid., 24.
311. "Williams College Ski Area," New England Lost Ski Areas Project, http://www.nelsap.org/ma/williamscollege.html.
312. Stevens, "Old Williams College Ski Area."
313. "Norseman's Hill," New England Lost Ski Areas Project, http://www. nelsap.org/ma/norsemans.html.
314. "Bolton," Ski Jumping Hill Archive, http://www.skisprungschanzen. com/EN/Ski+Jumps/USA-United+States/MA-Massachusetts/ Bolton/0707/.
315. "Norseman's Hill."
316. Ibid.
317. "Bolton."
318. Klaft, "(Ski) Jump Backward in Time."
319. "History Snippets: Skiing in Bolton," Wickedlocal.com, https://bolton. wickedlocal.com/article/20080125/NEWS/301259721.

320. "Norseman's Hill."

321. Hitchcock, "Remembering the Ski Jumps of South County."

322. "Ski Story," *Sandisfield Times* 1, no. 11 (March 2011).

323. Hitchcock, "Remembering the Ski Jumps of South County."

324. Drew, "Destined for Fame on Norwegian TV."

325. "Johanne Kolstad," Tri Corner News, January 25, 2012, https://tricornernews.com/johanne-kolstad-filmmakers-seek-info-famous-female-ski-jumper.

326. Hitchcock, "Remembering the Ski Jumps of South County."

327. "Ski Story."

328. Hitchcock, "Remembering the Ski Jumps of South County."

329. "Ski Story."

Vermont

330. "Hancock," Ski Jumping Hill Archive, http://www.skisprungschanzen.com/EN/Ski+Jumps/USA-United+States/VT-Vermont/Hancock/2427/.

331. *The Campus*, "Chipman Hill Ski Jumps."

332. "Middlebury College Snow Bowl," NewEnglandSkiHistory.com, https://www.newenglandskihistory.com/Vermont/middlebury.php.

333. *The Campus*, "Chipman Hill Ski Jumps."

334. Ibid.

335. Elkins, "Ski Slopes and Trails."

336. "Brief History and Timeline of the Middlebury College Snow Bowl."

337. *The Campus*, "Chipman Hill Ski Jumps."

338. "Brief History and Timeline of the Middlebury College Snow Bowl."

339. "Hancock."

340. "Our History," Middlebury Snow Bowl, https://www.middleburysnowbowl.com/about-us/.

341. "Norwich University Ski Area: Northfield, VT, 1939–1993," New England Lost Ski Areas Project, http://www.nelsap.org/vt/norwich.html.

342. "Norwich University Ski Area," NewEnglandSkiHistory.com, https://www.newenglandskihistory.com/Vermont/norwich.php.

343. Ibid.

344. "Fox Hill Ski Jump" Town of Franconia, http://www.franconianh.org/uploads/1/1/6/8/11680191/fox_hill_ski_jump.docx.

345. "Rochester Tow: Rochester, VT, Late 1930s– ?" New England Lost Ski Areas Project, http://www.nelsap.org/vt/rochester.html.

New Hampshire

346. Morgan, "Remembering the Dartmouth Ski Jump."
347. Ibid.
348. "History of the DOC," Dartmouth Outdoors, https://outdoors. dartmouth.edu/doc/history.html.
349. Harris, "Skiing over the New Hampshire Hills," 151–64.
350. "History of the DOC."
351. Harris, "Skiing over the New Hampshire Hills."
352. Chivers, "Old Days."
353. "History of the DOC."
354. "Otto Schniebs, 78, A Ski Instructor," *New York Times*, October 10, 1971.
355. "History of the DOC."
356. Winters, "'Pretty Spectacular Thing to See.'"
357. Morgan, "Remembering the Dartmouth Ski Jump."
358. Chivers, "Old Days."
359. Ibid.

New York

360. "South Colton Snow Bowl Presentation Planned," Adirondack Almanac, https://www.adirondackalmanack.com/2018/01/south-colton-snow-bowl-presentation-planned.html.
361. Jacques, "St. Lawrence Snow Bowl."
362. Ibid., 2.
363. Ibid., 8.
364. Ibid., 8.
365. Ibid., 2.
366. Ibid., 3.
367. Ibid., 3.
368. Elkins, "St. Lawrence Hill Will Open Today."
369. Axtell, "Remembering SLU's Snow Bowl."
370. Jacques, "St. Lawrence Snow Bowl," 5.
371. Ibid., 6.
372. "History of the Snowbowl," SLU Snowbowl, https://sites.google.com/site/slusnowbowlweb/history.
373. Axtell, "Remembering SLU's Snow Bowl."
374. Everts, "Remembering the Era of Downhill Skiing."

375. "Allegany," Ski Jumping Hill Archive, http://www.skisprungschanzen.com/ EN/Ski+Jumps/USA-United+States/NY-New+York/Allegany/0692/

376. Allegany State Park Historical Society, timeline, https://www.facebook. com/AlleganySPHS/.

377. Everts, "Remembering the Era of Downhill Skiing."

378. Ibid.

379. "Bear Mountain State Park," New York State: Parks, Recreation and Historic Preservation, https://parks.ny.gov/parks/bearmountain/details. aspx.

380. Leba, "Hudson Valley's Long-Lost Ski Areas (Revisited)"; Dechillo, "Ski Jumping Faces Long Decline."

381. "Bear Mountain," Ski Jumping Hill Archive, http://www. skisprungschanzen.com/EN/Ski+Jumps/USA-United+States/NY- New+York/Bear+Mountain/0700/.

382. Dechillo, "Ski Jumping Faces Long Decline."

383. Robinson, "USASJ Story Project."

384. Dechillo, "Ski Jumping Faces Long Decline."

385. Platt, "Ski Jumping over Downtown Rosendale."

386. Ibid.

387. "History," Ski the Gunks, http://www.skithegunks.com/new-page-4.

388. Platt, "Ski Jumping over Downtown Rosendale."

389. Ibid.

390. Michael Strauss, "Ski Jump Taken by Bringslimark."

391. "Rosendale:," Ski Jumping Hill Archive, http://www.skisprungschanzen. com/EN/Ski+Jumps/USA-United+States/NY-New+York/ Rosendale/2431/.

392. Platt, "Ski Jumping over Downtown Rosendale."

393. Ibid.

394. "Closest Thing We Had to the Olympics," Photo News, http://www. thephoto-news.com/news/the-closest-thing-we-had-to-the-olympics- CBPN20100212302129953.

395. Ibid.

396. Elkins, "Falkanger Leads Norway's Skiers."

397. "Olympic Members Vie In Ski Meet Near Poughkeepsie," *Vassar Chronicle* 7, no. 12 (January 1950).

398. "Closest Thing We Had to the Olympics."

399. "New York State Championship Ski Meet at Salisbury Mills," Getty Images, https://www.gettyimages.com/detail/video/on-skis-salisbury- mills-ny-ski-artists-take-chances-on-news-footage/591399128.

Maine

400. Breton, email, July 13, 2020.
401. "Century on Skis," New England Ski Museum, https://www. newenglandskimuseum.com/a-century-on-skis-chisholm-ski-club/.
402. Breton, email, July 13, 2020.
403. Ibid.
404. Ibid.
405. Ibid.
406. Elkins, "Blikstad Takes Class A Laurels."
407. Breton, email, July 13, 2020.
408. "Bethel," Ski Jumping Hill Archive, http://www.skisprungschanzen. com/EN/Ski+Jumps/USA-United+States/ME-Maine/Bethel/0704/.
409. "Gould Academy's Ski Area at Swan's Corner,'" Bethel Journals, http://www.thebetheljournals.info/SwansCornerJump.htm.
410. Remington and Remington, *We Jumped*, 49.
411. "Gould Academy's Ski Area at Swan's Corner."
412. Remington and Remington, *We Jumped*, 49.
413. "Gould Academy's Ski Area at Swan's Corner."
414. Remington and Remington, *We Jumped*, 56.
415. Ibid., 63, 65
416. Ibid., 66.
417. Pineland Ski & Outing Club, About, https://www.facebook.com/ Pineland-Ski-Outing-Club-766311350201819/about/?ref=page_ internal.
418. Remington and Remington, *We Jumped*, 27, 29.
419. Ibid., 37.
420. Ibid., 35.
421. Ibid., 35, 38.
422. Ibid., 37.
423. Ibid., 40.
424. Ibid., 45.
425. Ibid., 46.
426. Pineland Ski & Outing Club, private message, https://www.facebook. com/Pineland-Ski-Outing-Club-766311350201819/about/?ref=page_ internal.
427. Ibid.

Connecticut

428. Waldecker, ed., *Norfolk, Connecticut 1900–1975*.

429. Ibid.

430. "History," Norfolk Historical Society, https://norfolkhistoricalsociety. org/norfolk-history.

431. Waldecker, *Norfolk, Connecticut 1900–1975*.

432. Ibid.

433. Ibid.

434. Ibid.

435. Anson, *Jumping Through Time*, 71.

436. "Charles Everett Papers, Complete Text," Colebrook Historical Society, http://www.colebrookhistoricalsociety.org/PDF%20Images/Charles%20 Everett%20Papers,%20Complet.pdf.

437. Bob Grigg, "Bob's Bytes.".

438. Ibid.

439. Klaft, "(Ski) Jump Backward in Time."

440. "Charles Everett Papers, Complete Text."

441. DeLarm, *Colebrook Stories*, 107.

BIBLIOGRAPHY

Interviews and Correspondences

Breton, Dennis. Email message to author, July 13, 2020.

Burt, Jerry. Email to Tom Dodds, January 16, 2010, included in email correspondence between Tom Dodds and author, July 22, 2020.

Fiertz, Carey. Interview by the author, telephone, February 1, 2020.

Heistad, Erling. Interview by the author, telephone, February 17, 2020.

Jones, Chris. Interview by the author, Lake Placid, January 31, 2020.

Kiefer, Mat. Interview by the author, Salisbury, CT, February 12, 2020.

Letter from Ford Sayre Council to George T. Sayre, February 8, 1984. Included in email from Tom Dodds to author, July 22, 2020.

Levasseur, Mark. Interview by the author, telephone, December 21, 2019.

Malmquist, Walter. Email message to author, February 3, 2020.

————. Email message to author and "Eastern Jumps" spreadsheet attachment, April 5, 2020.

————. Interview by the author, telephone, February 4, 2020.

Norris, Tim. Personal communication with author, Andover, NH, July 8, 2020.

Picton, Mark. Interview by the author, telephone, February 3, 2020.

Stone, Larry. Interview by the author, telephone, March 3, 2020.

Tokle, Art. Interview by the author, telephone, February 25, 2020.

Newspaper Articles

Belson, Ken. "US in Nordic Combined: It's about Now." *New York Times*, February 16, 2014.

Bennington Banner. "Photos: The Hill Came Alive." February 17, 2020.

Branch, John. "It Seems Ski Jumping Has Become a Picnic." *New York Times*, February 23, 2010.

Brattleboro Reformer Historical Society. "Toboggan Slide Was Part of Winter Attraction." *Brattleboro Reformer*, February 7, 2020.

Butynski, Jason. "Jaywalking: Local Scene Once a Ski-Jumping Mecca." *Greenfield Reporter*, July 22, 2014.

Calamur, Krishnadev. "Why Norwegians Aren't Moving to the U.S." *The Atlantic*, January 12, 2018.

Dechillo, Suzanne. "Ski Jumping Faces Long Decline." *New York Times*, January 24, 1982.

Drew, Bernard A. "Destined for Fame on Norwegian TV." *Berkshire Eagle*, March 5, 2011.

Eastman, Tom. "Ski Jumping in the Valley: A Soaring Tradition." *Conway Daily Sun*, August 4, 2017.

Elkins, Frank. "Blikstad Takes Class A Laurels in Eastern Amateur Ski Jumping." *New York Times*, March 2, 1953.

———. "Falkanger Leads Norway's Skiers to Sweep of Top 4 Places in Jump." *New York Times*, January 23, 1950.

———. "Norwegian, Canadian and American Squads Compete In Ski Jumping Today." *New York Times*, January 8, 1950.

———. "Ski Curtain Rises: Big Show at Madison Square Garden to Mark the Opening of the New Season." *New York Times*, December 6, 1936.

———. "Ski Slopes and Trails." *New York Times*, December 14, 1949.

———. "St. Lawrence Hill Will Open Today." *New York Times*, January 14, 1951.

Fiertz, Carey. "View From the Top." *2018 Salisbury Ski Jumps 92nd Annual Jumpfest Program*, February 2018.

Fischel, Josh. "In Winter, Only in New Hampshire." *New York Times*, February 16, 2012.

Gibson, Owen. "Sochi 2014: Women Ski Jumpers Have Point to Prove after 90-Year Wait." *The Guardian*, February 10, 2014.

Gilbert, Caroline. "Lessons From My Son, a Ski Jumper." *2018 Salisbury Ski Jumps 92nd Annual Jumpfest Program*, February 2018.

Given, Karen. "Salisbury: 1 Town, 1 Ski Jump, 53 Junior Olympians." *WBUR Boston's NPR News Station*, February 26, 2011.

Grabel, Dan. "County Was a Ski-Jump Destination." *New York Times*, April 19, 1998.

Heath, Cindy. "A Winter Sports Legacy." *Lebanon Times*, January 22, 2015.

Hitchcock, John C. "College Racing: New Williams Area Offers Steep Slopes in Easy View." *Berkshire Eagle*, December 17, 1960.

Kobak, Annette. "No Man Is a Hero to His Sled Dogs." *New York Times*, May 16, 1999.

Koenig, H.P. "Cross-Country Ski Craze." *Chicago Tribune*, January 11, 1976.

Laconia Daily Sun. "Making the Jump—Plymouth Keeps High School Ski Jumping Alive in Lakes Region." December 11, 2015.

Mays, Chris. "Ski Jump Event a Family Effort." *Brattleboro Reformer*, February 12, 2020.

New York Times. "College Ski Title Won By Michelson." February 15, 1924.

———. "Dartmouth's Big Carnival." February 12, 1916.

———. "Dartmouth Takes Eastern Ski Title." February 25, 1968.

———. "In the Heart of the Adirondacks; More Strangers at Saranac Lake and Lake Placid Than Ever Before." July 9, 1893.

———. "Norwegians of Bay Ridge, a Proud and Tight-Knit Community." May 16, 1971.

———. "Otto Schniebs, 78, A Ski Instructor." October 10, 1971.

———. "Satre Takes Title with 152-Foot Leap." January 26, 1931.

———. "Seek to Aid Ski Jumper Under Death Sentence." March 28, 1930.

———. "Snow, Ice and Skis at Lake Placid Tomorrow: Hill Will Be 'Frozen' for Tomorrow's Holiday Jumping Meet." July 3, 1956.

———. "Summaries of Lake Placid Events." January 2, 1938.

———. "250 on Special Ski Train." December 27, 1938, accessed November 22, 2019.

———. "Winter's Splendor in the Adirondacks." December 17, 1916.

North Adams Transcript. "Williams Skiers Try New Jump." January 13, 1961.

Pegler, Westbrook. "Olympic Winter Games Open Today at Lake Placid." *Chicago Daily Tribune*, February 4, 1932.

Pennington, Bill. "The Ski Report; A Jumping Event Lands in Salisbury." *New York Times*, February 8, 2001.

———. "A Small Town's Leap of Faith." *New York Times*, February 8, 2011.

Reid, Nick. "Rebuilt by Bow Contractor, N.H.'s Famed Nansen Ski Jump to Host a Daring Last Hurrah." *Concord Monitor*, February 1, 2017.

Ridley, Jane. "Women Ski-Jumpers Take the Leap for First Time in 90 Years." *New York Post*, February 4, 2014.

Riley, Lori. "Salisbury's Ski Jumping Tradition Continues." *Hartford Courant*, February 20, 2011.

Schutz, John Patrick. "'Olympic Village' of Nyack." *Nyack News and Views*, February 19, 2014.

Stevens, Laura. "Old Williams College Ski Area a Fixable Mess." *Berkshire Eagle*. Accessed August 24, 2020.

Strauss, Michael. "Fall Kills U.S. Ski Jumper." *New York Times*, January 6, 1975.

———. "Kennedy Games at Lake Placid." *New York Times*, January 12, 1969.

———. "Ski Jump Honors Taken by Barber." *New York Times*, February 21, 1972.

———. "Ski-Jumping Won by Roy Sherwood." *New York Times*, January 6, 1964.

———. "Ski Jump Taken by Bringslimark; He Wins Combined Event at Curtailed Rosendale Meet." *New York Times*, January 31, 1966.

Sullivan, P.T. "Flying into the Night: A Thrilling Ride with NH's High School Jumpers." *New Hampshire Magazine*, January 2013.

Thibault, Amanda. "This Place in History: First Ski Tow in the U.S." *My Champlain Valley*, November 16, 2017.

Thomas, Katie. "After Long Fight for Inclusion, Women's Ski Jumping Gains Olympic Status." *New York Times*, April 7, 2011.

"Tim Norris: '66: Ski Jumping Hall of Fame." *The Dubliner*, Spring 2018.

Walden, Fred. "Williams Carnival Plunges on Despite Paucity of Snow." *Berkshire Eagle*, February 25, 1973.

Wallace, William N. "Coucheron Gains Ski-Jumping Title." *New York Times*, February 11, 1968.

Washington Post. "Lake Placid Awaits Rain, Cold Needed for Winter Olympics." January 16, 1932.

Zinser, Lynn. "American Wins Women's World Title." *New York Times*, February 21, 2009.

Secondary Works

Adirondack Almanac. "South Colton Snow Bowl Presentation Planned." January 12, 2018. Accessed July 10, 2020. https://www.adirondackalmanack.com/2018/01/south-colton-snow-bowl-presentation-planned.html.

Allegany State Park Historical Society. Timeline (Facebook Page). February 3, 2020. Accessed August 16, 2020, https://www.facebook.com/AlleganySPHS/.

Allen, E. John B. *From Skisport to Skiing: One Hundred Years of an American Sport.* Amherst: University of Massachusetts Press, 1993.

———. *Historical Dictionary of Skiing.* Lanham, MD: Scarecrow Press Inc., 2011.

Allen, Gary. *Memoir.* Gilford, NH: 1994.

Anson, Harold "Cork." *Jumping Through Time: A History of Ski Jumping in the United States and Southwest Canada.* Florence, OR: Port Hole Publications, 2010.

Ashburner, Tim. *The History of Ski Jumping.* Shrewsbury, UK: Quiller Press, 2003.

Axtell, Bob. "Remembering SLU's Snow Bowl as a State-of-the-Art Skiing Spot in the North Country." Interview by Todd Moe, North Country Public Radio. January 12, 2018. Audio. https://www.northcountrypublicradio.org/news/story/35426/20180112/remembering-slu-s-snow-bowl-as-a-state-of-the-art-skiing-spot-in-the-north-country.

Bays, Ted. *Nine Thousand Years of Skis: Norwegian Wood to French Plastic.* Ishpeming, MI: National Ski Hall of Fame Press, 1980.

The Bethel Journals. "Gould Academy's Ski Area at Swan's Corner: 'The First Sunday River Ski Area.'" Accessed September 2, 2020. http://www.thebetheljournals.info/SwansCornerJump.htm.

Boone, Chris. "New Hampshire Community Rallies to Save Historic Ski Jump." National Federation of State High School Associations. Accessed July 24, 2020. https://www.nfhs.org/articles/new-hampshire-community-rallies-to-save-historic-ski-jump/.

Brattleboro Outing Club. "The Genius, Genesis and Enduring Legacy of Fred Harris." Accessed July 14, 2020. https://brattleborooutingclub.org/wp-content/uploads/2020/04/history1.pdf.

———. "History." Accessed July 14, 2020. https://brattleborooutingclub.org/wp-content/uploads/2020/04/history2.pdf.

"Brief History and Timeline of the Middlebury College Snow Bowl." Special Collections & Archives, Davis Family Library, Middlebury College. Provided to author July 1, 2020, by Danielle Rougeau, Middlebury College Archivist.

Burns, Jay. "Video: Watch Ski Jumping off Mount David in 1936." Bates. Accessed February 28, 2020. https://www.bates.edu/news/2018/02/21/video-ski-jumping-off-mount-david-in-the-1930s/.

The Campus. "Chipman Hill Ski Jumps." Historical Timeline, Special Collections & Archives Davis Family Library, Middlebury College, 2013.

Provided to author July 1, 2020 by Danielle Rougeau, Middlebury College Archivist.

Cayton, Mary Kupiec, Elliot J. Gorn and Peter W. William, eds. *Encyclopedia of American Social History*. New York: Charles Scribner's Sons, 1993.

Chivers, Ted. "The Old Days." USA Nordic. Accessed July 14, 2020. https://www.usanordic.org/ted-chivers-24-dec-2017/.

Colebrook Historical Society. "Charles Everett Papers, Complete Text." Accessed September 8, 2020. http://www.colebrookhistoricalsociety.org/PDF%20Images/Charles%20Everett%20Papers,%20Complet.pdf.

Colorado Ski History. "Colorado Ski History Timeline 1900-1919." Accessed March 30, 2020. http://www.coloradoskihistory.com/history/timelines/1900.html.

Dartmouth Alumni. "Winter Carnival Posters." Pinterest. Accessed April 30, 2020. https://www.pinterest.com/dartmouthalumni/winter-carnival-posters/.

Dartmouth Outdoors. "History of the DOC." Accessed July 13, 2020. https://outdoors.dartmouth.edu/doc/history.html.

Davis, Jeremy K. *Lost Ski Areas of the Berkshires*. Charleston, SC: The History Press, 2018.

———. "Sharon Mountain Ski Area." New England Lost Ski Areas Project. Last modified December 23, 2006. Accessed March 30, 2020. http://www.nelsap.org/ct/sharon.html.

DeLarm, Alan. *Colebrook Stories*. Colebrook, CT: Colebrook Historical Society, 1979: 107. https://books.google.com/books/about/Colebrook_stories.html?id=Xf0nAQAAMAAJ.

Denning, Andrew. *Skiing into Modernity: A Cultural and Environmental History*. Oakland: University of California Press, 2015.

Erwin, Katharine. "Salisbury, Connecticut's Jumpfest 2015." Cool Hunting. February 10, 2015. Accessed March 3, 2020. https://coolhunting.com/culture/jumpfest-connecticut-2015/.

Everts, Deb. "Remembering the Era of Downhill Skiing and Jumping at Allegany State Park." *Salamanca Press*, January 20, 2016. Accessed August 16, 2020. http://www.salamancapress.com/news/remembering-the-era-of-downhill-skiing-and-jumping-at-allegany-state-park/article_f93f2bf4-bf91-11e5-a3cb-3b81225ceb44.html.

Final Report: XIII Olympic Winter Games, Lake Placid, N.Y., February 13–24, 1980. XIII Olympic Winter Games Committee: Lake Placid, NY, 1980. Accessed July 12, 2020. https://digital.la84.org/digital/collection/p17103coll8/id/30858.

Ford K. Sayre Memorial Ski Council. "Ford Sayre History." Included in email correspondence between Tom Dodds and author, July 22, 2020.

———. "Ski Jumping." Accessed August 3, 2020. https://www.fordsayre. org/nordic/jumping/.

Fry, John. *The Story of Modern Skiing.* Lebanon, NH: University Press of New England, 2006.

Gasser, Hans-Heini (SUI). "Jumping Hills Construction Norm 2018 Implementing Provisions for Art. 411 of the ICR Ski Jumping." International Ski Federation. Accessed March 25, 2020. https://assets. fis-ski.com/image/upload/v1592381507/fis-prod/assets/Construction-Norm_2018-2.pdf.

Getty Images. "New York State Championship Ski Meet at Salisbury Mills." January 1, 1934. Accessed July 2, 2020. https://www.gettyimages.com/ detail/video/on-skis-salisbury-mills-ny-ski-artists-take-chances-on-news-footage/591399128.

Gildea, Dennis. "Dartmouth and the Debate Over Ski Jumping in NCAA Competition." *Journal of Intercollegiate Sport* 2 (2009): 286–98.

Grigg, Bob. "Bob's Bytes." Colebrook Historical Society. Accessed September 8, 2020. http://www.colebrookhistoricalsociety.org/PDF%20Images/ Colebrook%20River%20Recreation.pdf.

Hamlin, Katie. "Winter Carnival Photo Gallery: Skiing, Skating, and Sport." Dartmouth. Accessed April 27, 2020. https://250.dartmouth. edu/news/2019/02/winter-carnival-photo-gallery-skiing-skating-and-sport.

Hanson, J. "Recreation Movement in the United States." Virginia Commonwealth University. Accessed November 22, 2019. https:// socialwelfare.library.vcu.edu/youth/recreation-movement-in-the-united-states/.

Harris, Fred H. "Skiing Over The New Hampshire Hills." *National Geographic*, February 1920. Accessed July 13, 2020. http://www.hampton.lib.nh.us/ nhskiing/nhhills.htm.

Harris Hill Ski Jump. "Frequently Asked Questions." Accessed July 14, 2020. https://harrishillskijump.com.

Hinkley, Jed. "A Legend Retires but the Future Is Bright." USA Nordic. Accessed July 24, 2020. https://www.usanordic.org/a-legend-retires-but-the-future-is-bright/.

Hinkley, Jed, and Jeff Hastings. USA Nordic Documents. "US Athlete Participation 2018/19." Spring Summit 2019. Accessed March 25, 2020. https://www.usanordic.org/who-we-are/documents/.

"History Snippets: Skiing in Bolton." Wickedlocal.com. January 25, 2008. Accessed August 20, 2020. https://bolton.wickedlocal.com/article/20080125/NEWS/301259721.

Hitchcock, John. "Remembering the Ski Jumps of South County." iBerkshires.com. Accessed August 20, 2020. https://www.iberkshires.com/story/12988/Remembering-the-ski-jumps-of-South-County.html.

Hunsaker, Hannah, and Will Kannegieser. "A History of Recreational Skiing in the Northern Berkshires." History paper, Williams College, 2019, 13. Accessed August 24, 2020. Provided to author by Sarah Currie of the Williamstown Historical Museum.

Huntford, Roland. *Two Planks and a Passion: The Dramatic History of Skiing.* New York: Continuum, 2008.

Jacques, Thatcher. "St. Lawrence Snow Bowl." St. Lawrence Archives. Accessed July 10, 2020. Provided to author by Paul Haggett, Special Collections Technician at St. Lawrence Archives.

Jumpfest. "Salisbury Invitational Ski Jumping." Accessed March 10, 2020. http://www.jumpfest.org/.

Kimball Union Academy. "Charles Mallett '41, Roland Tremblay '51 and John Kluge '66 Were Honored at Reunion 2006." Accessed July 13, 2020. https://www.kua.org/news-detail?pk=276740.

Klaft, Lynne. "A (Ski) Jump Backward in Time." Telegram.com. March 22, 2007. Accessed August 20, 2020. https://www.telegram.com/article/20070322/MONTY/703220309.

Lattimer, George M. *III Olympic Winter Games Lake Placid 1932 Official Report.* Lake Placid, NY: III Olympic Winter Games Committee, 1932. Accessed July 12, 2020. https://web.archive.org/web/20080410085042/http://www.la84foundation.org/6oic/OfficialReports/1932/1932w.pdf.

Leba, Jennifer. "The Hudson Valley's Long-Lost Ski Areas (Revisited)." *Hudson Valley*, December 2007. Accessed August 2, 2020. https://hvmag.com/life-style/the-hudson-valleys-long-lost-ski-areas-revisited/.

Leich, Jeff. "Green Mountains, White Gold: Origins of Vermont Skiing: Brattleboro: Center of All Aspects of Skiing." *Journal of the New England Ski Museum* 94 (Summer 2014).

———. "Nordic Skiing from Stone Age to Skating: Part Two: Glory Days of American Skisport." *Journal of the New England Ski Museum* 76 (Winter 2010).

Lund, Morten. "The 1930s: The Unexpected Blossoming of Alpine Skiing." International Skiing History Association. Accessed March 30, 2020. https://skiinghistory.org/gallery/1930s-unexpected-blossoming-alpine-skiing.

Macarthur, Paul J. "Taking Flight: The Evolution of Ski Flying, From the First Recorded Jump to the Latest World Record." *Skiing Heritage Journal* 23, no. 2 (March–April 2011): 20–25.

Maine: An Encyclopedia. "Rumford." Accessed July 28, 2020. https://maineanencyclopedia.com/rumford/.

Manchester, Lee, ed. *The Lake Placid Club, 1890–2002.* Jay, NY: Makebelieve Publishing, 2008. https://www.slideshare.net/LeeManchester/the-lake-placid-club-1890-2002.

Marcus, Heather. "Salisbury, Connecticut Photographs." New England Today Travel. October 16, 2015. Accessed April 28, 2020. https://newengland.com/today/travel/connecticut/salisbury-connecticut-photographs/.

McPhaul, Meghan McCarthy. "Berlin's Nansen Ski Jump Looks to 2020 Competition." *New Hampshire Union Leader*, February 12, 2019. Accessed June 22, 2020. https://www.unionleader.com/news/berlin-s-nansen-ski-jump-looks-to-2020-competition/article_42279e6f-db06-5e62-b553-849f8fe4cbf1.html.

———. "The Big Nansen: Berlin, New Hampshire's Legendary Jump Poised for a Comeback." *Journal of the New England Ski Museum* 107 (Winter 2018).

Merriam-Webster Dictionary. "Skimeister." Accessed February 18, 2020. https://www.merriam-webster.com/dictionary/skimeister.

Middlebury Snow Bowl. "Our History." Accessed August 1, 2020. https://www.middleburysnowbowl.com/about-us/.

Miller, Dave. "Jim McKay: The Thrill of Victory…The Agony of Defeat." Bleacher Report. June 14, 2008. Accessed February 18, 2020. https://bleacherreport.com/articles/29612-jim-mckay-the-thrill-of-victorythe-agony-of-defeat.

Morgan, Evan. "Remembering the Dartmouth Ski Jump: 1929–1993." *The Dartmouth.* February 20, 2017. Accessed July 13, 2020. https://www.thedartmouth.com/article/2017/02/remembering-the-dartmouth-ski-jump-1929-1993.

Nadeau, Walter. "Nansen Ski Club and Ski Jump." Pdf included in email correspondence between Walter Nadeau and author. June 14, 2020.

"Nansen Ski Jump Named to National Register." *Business NH Magazine*, July 2019. Accessed March 25, 2020. https://www.businessnhmagazine.com/article/nansen-ski-jump-named-to-national-register.

National Park Service. "Quick History of the National Park Service." Last modified May 14, 2018. Accessed November 22, 2019. https://www.nps.gov/articles/quick-nps-history.htm.

———. "Yellowstone: History and Culture." Last modified September 18, 2019. Accessed November 22, 2019. https://www.nps.gov/yell/learn/historyculture/index.htm.

New England Lost Ski Areas Project. "Norseman's Hill: Bolton, MA 1950–1957." Accessed August 26, 2020. http://www.nelsap.org/ma/norsemans.html.

———. "Norwich University Ski Area: Northfield, VT, 1939–1993." Accessed August 28, 2020. http://www.nelsap.org/vt/norwich.html.

———. "Oak Hill Hanover, NH." Accessed July 20, 2020. http://www.nelsap.org/nh/oakhill.html.

———. "Rochester Tow: Rochester, VT, Late 1930s– ?" Accessed July 30, 2020. http://www.nelsap.org/vt/rochester.html.

———. "Williams College Ski Area: Williamstown, MA, 1960–Mid 1970s." Accessed August 24, 2020. http://www.nelsap.org/ma/williamscollege.html.

New England Ski History. "Middlebury College Snow Bowl." Accessed August 2, 2020. https://www.newenglandskihistory.com/Vermont/middlebury.php.

———. "Norwich University Ski Area." Accessed August 28, 2020. https://www.newenglandskihistory.com/Vermont/norwich.php.

———. "Stowe Mountain Resort." September 25, 2019. Accessed March 30, 2020. https://www.newenglandskihistory.com/Vermont/stowe.php.

New England Ski Museum. "A Century on Skis: Chisholm Ski Club." Product Description. Accessed July 28, 2020. https://www.newenglandskimuseum.com/a-century-on-skis-chisholm-ski-club/.

New Hampshire State Parks. "Nansen Ski Jump Restoration Project." Accessed March 25, 2020. https://www.nhstateparks.org/news-events/improving-state-parks/nansen-ski-jump-restoration-project.

Newport Recreation Department. "Roland Tremblay Ski Jump Complex." Accessed July 27, 2020. http://www.newportrec.com/index.php?n=roland_tremblay_ski_jump_complex.

New York State: Parks, Recreation and Historic Preservation. "Bear Mountain State Park." Accessed August 2, 2020. https://parks.ny.gov/parks/bearmountain/details.aspx.

NH Gives. "Nansen Ski Club Inc." Accessed July 21, 2020. https://www.nhgives.org/organizations/nansen-ski-club-inc.

Norfolk Historical Society. "History." Accessed September 6, 2020. https://norfolkhistoricalsociety.org/norfolk-history.

Nybelius, Marit Stub, and Annette R. Hofmann, ed. *License to Jump! A Story of Women's Ski Jumping.* Falun, Sweden: Scandbook, 2015.

Olympic Games. "Nordic Combined." Accessed March 2, 2020. https://www.olympic.org /vancouver-2010/nordic-combined.

———. "Normal Hill Individual Men." Accessed March 2, 2020. https://www. olympic.org/ chamonix-1924/ski-jumping/normal-hill-individual-men.

———. "Ski Jumping." Accessed March 3, 2020. https://www.olympic. org/ski-jumping.

———. "Winter Games." Accessed March 3, 2020. https://www.olympic. org/winter-games.

"Olympic Members Vie in Ski Meet Near Poughkeepsie." *Vassar Chronicle* 7, no. 12 (January 1950). Accessed July 2, 2020. https://newspaperarchives. vassar.edu/?a=d&d=vcchro19500121-01.2.26.

Orlowski, Frank. "Storrs Hill Ski Area a Community Tradition Lives On." *Lebanon Times* (Fall 2017). Accessed June 20, 2020.http://docplayer.net/60498400- There-are-brave-people-in-the-world-who-willingly-put.html.

The Photo News. "The Closest Thing We Had to the Olympics." February 22, 2012. Accessed July 2, 2020. http://www.thephoto-news.com/news/ the-closest-thing-we-had-to-the-olympics-CBPN201002123022129953.

Pineland Ski & Outing Club. About (Facebook Page). Accessed September 2, 2020. https://www.facebook.com/Pineland-Ski-Outing- Club-766311350201819/about/?ref=page_internal.

———. Private Message (Facebook Page). Accessed September 2, 2020. https:// www.facebook.com/Pineland-Ski-Outing-Club-766311350201819/

Platt, Frances Marion. "Ski Jumping Over Downtown Rosendale: A History." hv1. January 24, 2019. Accessed July 2, 2020. https://hudsonvalleyone. com/2019/01/24/ski-jumping-over-downtown-rosendale-a-history/.

Proctor. "Ski Jumping at Proctor." Accessed July 23, 2020. https://www. proctoracademy.org/on-campus/athletics/proctor-on-snow/ski-jumping.

Ready to Fly. Directed by William Kerig. Scott A. Zeller, Whitney Childers, 2012. Amazon Prime.

Remington, Robert Lee, and Thomas K. Remington. *We Jumped*. Self- published, 2015.

Republican American Archives. "Roy R. Sherwood." October 23, 2017. Accessed June 20, 2020. https://archives.rep-am.com/2017/10/23/roy- r-sherwood/.

Robinson, Dave. "USASJ Story Project 13-DEC-2014 Dave Robinson." USA Nordic. December 13, 2014. Accessed August 2, 2020. https:// www.usanordic.org/usasj-story-project-13-dec-2014-dave-robinson/.

Rosin, Skip. "Their Rejection, Our Loss." *Wall Street Journal*, February 10, 2010. Accessed March 5, 2020. https://www.wsj.com/articles/SB10001 424052748704533204575047482012978 218.

"Roy Sherwood 1932–2017." *2018 Salisbury Ski Jumps 92nd Annual Jumpfest Program*, February 2018.

Rybczynski, Witold. *A Clearing in the Distance: Frederick Law Olmsted and America in the Nineteenth Century.* New York: Scribner, 1999.

"Salisbury Is Still Jumping." Salisbury Association display panel pdf included in email correspondence between Louis J. Bucceri and author. June 17, 2020.

Ski Jumping Hill Archive. "Allegany: Allegany State Park Ski Jump." Accessed August 16, 2020. http://www.skisprungschanzen.com/EN/Ski+Jumps/ USA-United+States/NY-New+York/Allegany/0692/.

———. "Bear Mountain." Accessed August 2, 2020. http://www. skisprungschanzen.com/EN/Ski+Jumps/USA-United+States/NY-New+York/Bear+Mountain/0700/.

———. "Bethel: Sunday River Ski Jumps." Accessed September 2, 2020. http:// www.skisprungschanzen.com/EN/Ski+Jumps/USA-United+States/ME-Maine/Bethel/0704/.

———. "Bolton: Norseman's Hill." Accessed August 26, 2020. http:// www.skisprungschanzen.com/EN/Ski+Jumps/USA-United+States/ MA-Massachusetts/Bolton/0707/.

———. "Hancock: Edward Cignac Memorial Ski Jump." Accessed August 2, 2020. http://www.skisprungschanzen.com/EN/Ski+Jumps/USA-United+States/VT-Vermont/Hancock/2427/.

———. "Lake Placid: MacKenzie Intervale Ski Jumping Complex." Accessed July 12, 2020. http://www.skisprungschanzen.com/EN/ Ski+Jumps/USA-United+States/NY-New+York/Lake+Placid/0576-MacKenzie+Intervale+Ski+Jumping+Complex/.

———. "Massachusetts." Accessed March 30, 2020. http://www. skisprungschanzen.com/EN/Ski+Jumps/USA-United+States/MA-Massachusetts/.

———. "Rosendale: Joppenbergh Mountain Ski Jump." Accessed July 2, 2020. http://www.skisprungschanzen.com/EN/Ski+Jumps/USA-United+States/NY-New+York/Rosendale/2431/.

"Ski Jumping Comes to Salisbury." Salisbury Association display panel PDF included in email correspondence between Louis J. Bucceri and author. June 17, 2020.

"Ski Story: Film Makers Come to Town." *Sandisfield Times* 1, no. 11 (March 2011). Accessed August 21, 2020. https://www.sandisfieldtimes.org/ Sandisfield_Times_2011-03.pdf.

Ski the Gunks. "History." Accessed July 2, 2020. http://www.skithegunks. com/new-page-4.

Slack, Bill. "Williams Outing Club: History." Williams. Accessed August 24, 2020. https://woc.williams.edu/about-woc/history/.

SLU Snowbowl. "History of the Snowbowl." Accessed July 10, 2020. https://sites.google.com/site/slusnowbowlweb/history.

Sprague, Dana. "History Timeline." Harris Hill Ski Jump. Accessed November 22, 2019. https://harrishillskijump.com/history/.

Stepp, Morgan. "Gene Ross Memorial Ski Jump." iPetitions. November 11, 2015. Accessed July 24, 2020. https://www.ipetitions.com/petition/gene-ross-memorial-ski-jump.

Town of Franconia. "Fox Hill Ski Jump." Accessed July 30, 2020. http://www.franconianh.org/uploads/1/1/6/8/11680191/fox_hill_ski_jump.docx.

Town of Newport, New Hampshire. "Historical Chronology of Newport." Accessed July 27, 2020. https://www.newportnh.gov/sites/g/files/vyhlif4776/f/uploads/historical_chronology_story.pdf.

Tri Corner News. "Johanne Kolstad: Filmmakers Seek Info on Famous Female Ski Jumper." January 25, 2012. Accessed August 21, 2020. https://tricornernews.com/johanne-kolstad-filmmakers-seek-info-famous-female-ski-jumper.

USA Nordic. "Tara Geraghty-Moats." Accessed March 25, 2020. https://www.usanordic.org/national-teams/women-ski-jumping/tara-geraghty-moats/.

US Ski and Snowboard Hall of Fame. "Erling Heistad: Hall of Fame Class of 1966." Accessed June 17, 2020. https://skihall.com/hall-of-famers/erling-heistad/#:~:text=Erling%20Heistad%20was%20elected%20to,25%20and%2050%20meter%20hills.

Vintage Postcards and Collectibles. "Highest Ski Jump in the United States." Accessed March 25, 2020. https://www.cardcow.com/708596/berlin-new-hampshire-highest-ski-jump-united-states/.

Waldecker, Alice V., ed. *Norfolk, Connecticut 1900–1975*. Winsted, CT: Winchester Press, 1976.

Wallen, Joan. "Andover's Little League of Skiing: How a small town produces champion skiers." *Kearsage Magazine*, Winter 2009–10.

Ward, Grace. "A Jump above the Rest." Ski NH. December 31, 2018. Accessed July 24, 2020. https://www.skinh.com/blog/A-Jump-Above-the-Rest.

Waterman, Laura, and Guy Waterman. *Forest and Crag: A History of Hiking, Trail Blazing, and Adventure in the Northeast Mountains*. Boston: Appalachian Mountain Club, 1989.

Wikipedia. "Sondre Norheim." Accessed April 27, 2020. https://en.wikipedia.org/wiki/Sondre_Norheim.

Winters, Mary. "'A Pretty Spectacular Thing to See': Carnival Ski Jumps." *The Dartmouth*, February 8, 2019. Accessed July 14, 2020. https://www. thedartmouth.com/article/2019/02/winters-ski-jumps.

Women's Ski Jumping USA. "Our Olympic Story." Accessed February 25, 2020. http://www.wsjusa.com /olympic-inclusion.

Zehner, Jacki. "Sochi 2014—Women Ski Jumpers Are Ready to Fly." Linkedin. February 7, 2014. Accessed April 27, 2020. https://www. linkedin.com/pulse/20140207195238-25295057-sochi-2014-women-ski-jumpers-are-ready-to-fly.

ABOUT THE AUTHOR

Ariel Kobayashi grew up in Washington, Connecticut, and learned to ski jump at the age of nine in Salisbury, Connecticut. As the jumping coach at Salisbury Winter Sports Association from 2016 to 2020, she accompanied eastern jumpers to the Junior Nationals in Chicago and Anchorage and spearheaded a major upgrade to the twenty-meter ski jump in Salisbury.

Ariel worked in the ski industry in Alta, Utah; Squaw Valley, California; and the Mad River Valley in Vermont before returning to college where she graduated summa cum laude from SUNY Purchase with a degree in history. Her Senior Project, which was the backbone of this book, received the Richard Maas Prize in American History.

Visit us at
www.historypress.com